Collins
My First
English-English-Gujarati
Dictionary
અંગ્રેજી-અંગ્રેજી-ગુજરાતી

Exclusively Distributed in the Indian subcontinent by Ratna Sagar

HarperCollins Publishers
Westerhill Road
Bishopbriggs
Glasgow
G64 2QT

First edition 2011

Reprint 10 9 8 7 6 5 4 3 2 1 0

© HarperCollins Publishers 2011

ISBN   978-0-00-743861-7

Collins® is a registered trademark of
HarperCollins Publishers Limited

www.collinslanguage.com

A catalogue record for this book is available
from the British Library

Artwork and design by Q2A Media

Printed in India by Gopsons Papers Ltd

Images used under licence from
Shutterstock.com

All rights reserved. No part of this book may
be reproduced, stored in a retrieval system,
or transmitted in any form or by any means,
electronic, mechanical, photocopying,
recording or otherwise, without the prior
permission in writing of the Publisher. This
book is sold subject to the conditions that
it shall not, by way of trade or otherwise, be
lent, re-sold, hired out or otherwise circulated
without the publisher's prior consent in any
form of binding or cover other than that in
which it is published and without a similar
condition including this condition being
imposed on the subsequent purchaser.

Entered words that we have reason to believe
constitute trademarks have been designated
as such. However, neither the presence
nor absence of such designation should be
regarded as affecting the legal status of any
trademark.

Editorial Consultant
Shilpa Das
National Institute of Design, India

Translation Co-ordinator
Ajit Shirodkar
Shakti Enterprise

Translators
Hemadri Shah
Vimal Panchal
N.D. Modha

Computing Support
Thomas Callan

Editors
Gerry Breslin
Freddy Chick
Lucy Cooper
Kerry Ferguson

Editor-in-chief
Dr Elaine Higgleton

આ શબ્દકોશમાં શબ્દ કઈ રીતે શોધવું

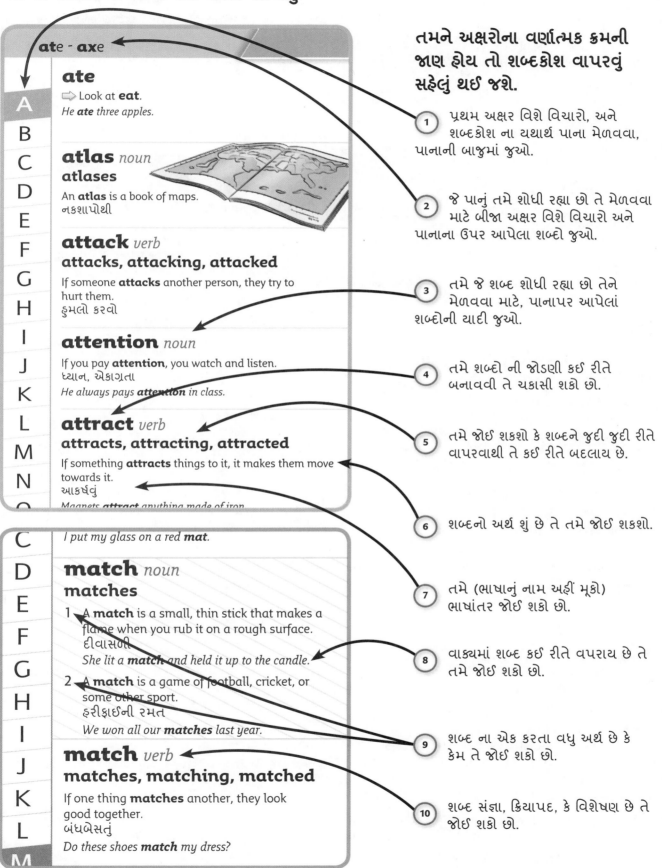

ate - axe

A

ate
➡ Look at **eat**.
*He **ate** three apples.*

atlas *noun*
atlases
An **atlas** is a book of maps.
નકશાપોથી

attack *verb*
attacks, attacking, attacked
If someone **attacks** another person, they try to hurt them.
હુમલો કરવો

attention *noun*
If you pay **attention**, you watch and listen.
ધ્યાન, એકાગ્રતા
*He always pays **attention** in class.*

attract *verb*
attracts, attracting, attracted
If something **attracts** things to it, it makes them move towards it.
આકર્ષવું
*Magnets **attract** anything made of iron*

B C D E F G H I J K L M N O

---

*I put my glass on a red **mat**.*

match *noun*
matches
1 A **match** is a small, thin stick that makes a flame when you rub it on a rough surface.
દીવાસળી
*She lit a **match** and held it up to the candle.*

2 A **match** is a game of football, cricket, or some other sport.
હરીફાઈની રમત
*We won all our **matches** last year.*

match *verb*
matches, matching, matched
If one thing **matches** another, they look good together.
બંધબેસતું
*Do these shoes **match** my dress?*

C D E F G H I J K L M

તમને અક્ષરોના વર્ણાત્મક ક્રમની જાણ હોય તો શબ્દકોશ વાપરવું સહેલું થઈ જશે.

1 પ્રથમ અક્ષર વિશે વિચારો, અને શબ્દકોશ ના યથાર્થ પાના મેળવવા, પાનાની બાજુમાં જુઓ.

2 જે પાનું તમે શોધી રહ્યા છો તે મેળવવા માટે બીજા અક્ષર વિશે વિચારો અને પાનાના ઉપર આપેલા શબ્દો જુઓ.

3 તમે જે શબ્દ શોધી રહ્યા છો તેને મેળવવા માટે, પાનાપર આપેલાં શબ્દોની યાદી જુઓ.

4 તમે શબ્દો ની જોડણી કઈ રીતે બનાવવી તે ચકાસી શકો છો.

5 તમે જોઈ શકશો કે શબ્દને જુદી જુદી રીતે વાપરવાથી તે કઈ રીતે બદલાય છે.

6 શબ્દનો અર્થ શું છે તે તમે જોઈ શકશો.

7 તમે (ભાષાનું નામ અહીં મૂકો) ભાષાંતર જોઈ શકો છો.

8 વાક્યમાં શબ્દ કઈ રીતે વપરાય છે તે તમે જોઈ શકો છો.

9 શબ્દ ના એક કરતા વધુ અર્થ છે કે કેમ તે જોઈ શકો છો.

10 શબ્દ સંજ્ઞા, ક્રિયાપદ, કે વિશેષણ છે તે જોઈ શકો છો.

શબ્દો કઈ રીતે માફક આવે છે

સંજ્ઞાઓ

જે શબ્દો વ્યક્તિઓ, સ્થાન કે વસ્તુઓ દર્શાવે તેઓને **સંજ્ઞા** કહેવાય છે.

> **arm** *noun*
> **bird** *noun*
> **car** *noun*

કોઈ વસ્તુ એક થી વધુ સંખ્યામાં હોય તો એ શબ્દ વાપરવો જેને અંતે –s હોય.

> **arms**
> **birds**
> **cars**

વિશેષણ

વ્યક્તિઓ, સ્થાન કે વસ્તુઓ કેવાં છે તે **વિશેષણ** દર્શાવે છે.

> **happy** *adjective*
> **wild** *adjective*
> **wet** *adjective*

વિશેષણોને જુદી જુદી રીતે વાપરી શકાય છે.

> **happier, happiest**
> **wilder, wildest**
> **wetter, wettest**

ક્રિયાપદ

તમે જે કાર્યો કરો છો તેનું વર્ણન **ક્રિયાપદ** કરે છે.

> **eat** *verb*
> **cry** *verb*
> **talk** *verb*

ક્રિયાપદો ને જુદી જુદી રીતે વાપરી શકાય છે.

> **eats, eating, ate, eaten**
> **cries, crying, cried**
> **talks, talking, talked**

તમે હાલમાં જે કાર્યો કરી રહ્યા છો તેઓને **ક્રિયાપદ** દર્શાવે છે.

> *He **teaches** people how to play the piano.*
> *He **is** in the school football team.*

ભૂતકાળમાં તમે જે કાર્યો કર્યા છે તેઓને ક્રિયાપદ દર્શાવે છે.

> *She **took** the plates into the kitchen.*
> *She **talked** to him on the phone.*

ભવિષ્યમાં તમે જે કાર્યો કરશો તેઓને દર્શાવવા માટે પણ ક્રિયાપદ વાપરી શકાય છે.

> *Mum **will** be angry.*
> *Our teacher **will** give the prizes to the winners.*
> ***We'll** come along later.*

જોડણી ના નિષ્ણાત બનવા માટેની વિશિષ્ટ સૂચનાઓ!

શબ્દકોશ માં જોઈતો શબ્દ મળ્યા બાદ, એની જોડણી કઈ રીતે લખવી તે શીખવા માટે "Look, Say, Cover, Write, Check" ની તરકીબ વાપરો:

Look શબ્દને ધ્યાનથી જુઓ.
તેના દેખાવ તથા લંબાઈ ને જુઓ.
તેમા આવેલાં અક્ષરોને જુઓ કે તે અક્ષરો ના કોઈ પેટર્ન છે જે તમને ભવિષ્યમાં એની જોડણી યાદ કરાવવામાં મદદ કરી શકે, દા.ત. બ્રાઈટ, લાઈટ, ટાઈટ.

Say શબ્દને મોટેથી ઉચ્ચારો.
શબ્દની ધ્વની વિષે વિચારો! તમે બીજા કોઈ શબ્દ ની જોડણી વિષે જાણો છો જની ધ્વની આના જેવી હોય? તમારા શબ્દમાં આના જેવી ધ્વની પેટન છે? શબ્દનું ઉચ્ચારણ કરો અને એની જોડણી ને લખવાનો પ્રયાસ કરો.

Cover શબ્દને એવી રીતે ઢાંકો કે તમે એને જોઈ ન શકો.

Write શબ્દકોશમાં જોયા વગર શબ્દને લખીલો. આવું કરતી વખતે શબ્દ કેવો દેખાય છે તે વિષે વિચારો. એ બરાબર લાગે છે કે નહી? તેનો આકાર બરાબર છે? તેની લંબાઈ બરાબર લાગે છે?

Check તમે તેને સાચી રીતે લખ્યું છે કે નહીં તે તપાસો.

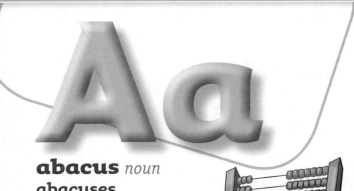

Aa

abacus *noun*
abacuses

An **abacus** is a frame with beads that move along pieces of wire. It is used for counting.
સંખ્યા ગણવા વપરાતી મણકાની ઘોડી

able

If you are **able** to do something, you know how to do it.
શક્તિવાળું, સમર્થ
*She is **able** to swim.*

about

1 **About** means to do with.
-ના વિષે
*This book is **about** history.*

2 **About** also means near to something.
લગભગ, આશરે
*His grandfather is **about** 80 years old.*

above

If something is **above** another thing, it is over it or higher than it.
ઉપર
*Lift the ball **above** your head.*

accident *noun*
accidents

1 An **accident** is something nasty that happens, and that hurts someone.
અકસ્માત
*He broke his leg in a car **accident**.*

2 If something happens by **accident**, you do not expect it to happen.
અજાણપણે કરેલું કૃત્ય
*I dropped a cup by **accident**.*

ache *verb*
aches, aching, ached

If a part of your body **aches**, you feel a steady pain there.
દુ:ખવું
*My leg **aches** a lot.*

acorn *noun*
acorns

An **acorn** is the seed of an oak tree.
એક વૃક્ષનું ફળ

across

If someone goes **across** a place, they go from one side of it to the other.
એક બાજુથી બીજી બાજુ સુધી, સોંસરું,આરપાર
*She walked **across** the road.*

act *verb*
acts, acting, acted

1 When you **act**, you do something.
કાર્ય કરવું
*The police **acted** quickly to stop the fight.*

2 If you **act** in a play or film, you pretend to be one of the people in it.
ભાગ ભજવવો, પાત્ર ભજવવું

active *adjective*

Someone who is **active** moves around a lot.
સક્રિય: ઉત્સાહી
*My grandmother is very **active** for her age.*

add *verb*
adds, adding, added

1 If you **add** one thing to another, you put it with the other thing.
ઉમેરવું
Add the water to the flour.

2 If you **add** numbers together, you find out how many they make together.
વધારવું, ઉમેરવું
Add three and six.

address *noun*
addresses

Your **address** is the name of the place where you live.
સરનામું

adjective *noun*
adjectives

An **adjective** is a word like "big" or "beautiful", that tells you more about a person or thing.
વિશેષણ

a
b
c
d
e
f
g
h
i
j
k
l
m
n
o
p
q
r
s
t
u
v
w
x
y
z

1

A
B
C
D
E
F
G
H
I
J
K
L
M
N
O
P
Q
R
S
T
U
V
W
X
Y
Z

admire *verb*
admires, admiring, admired

If you **admire** something, you like it and think that it is very nice or very good.
પ્રશંસા કરવી
I admired his painting.

adopt *verb*
adopts, adopting, adopted

If you **adopt** another person's child, you take them into your own family as your son or daughter.
દત્તક લેવું

adult *noun*
adults

An **adult** is a person who is not a child anymore.
વયસ્ક

adventure *noun*
adventures

An **adventure** is something exciting which you do, or which happens to you.
સાહસ, જોખમી કામ
He wrote a book about his adventures in the jungle.

adverb *noun*
adverbs

An **adverb** is a word like "slowly", "now", or "very" that tells you about how something is done.
ક્રિયાવિશેષણ

aeroplane *noun*
aeroplanes

An **aeroplane** is a large vehicle with wings and engines that flies through the air.
હવાઈજહાજ

afraid *adjective*

If you are **afraid**, you are frightened because you think that something bad will happen to you.
ભયભીત, ડરેલું
I am not afraid of the dark.

after

1   If something happens **after** another thing, it happens later than it.
    પછીથી
    I watched television after dinner.

2   If you go **after** a person or thing, you follow them or chase them.
    પાછળ
    They ran after her.

afternoon *noun*
afternoons

The **afternoon** is the part of each day between twelve noon and about six o'clock.
બપોરથી સાંજ સુધીનો સમય, દિવસનો પાછલો પહોર

again

If something happens **again**, it happens another time.
ફરીથી
We went to the park again yesterday.

against

1   If something is **against** another thing, it is touching it.
    અઢેલીને, ટેકીને
    He leaned against the wall.

2   If you play **against** someone in a game, you try to beat them.
    -ની વિરુદ્ધમાં
    The two teams played against one another.

age *noun*
ages

Your **age** is the number of years that you have lived.
વય, ઉંમર

ago

You use **ago** to talk about a time in the past.
પૂર્વે, અગાઉ
She left two weeks ago.

agree *verb*
agrees, agreeing, agreed
If you **agree** with someone, you think the same as they do about something.
સંમત થવું
*I **agree** with you about him.*

ahead
Someone who is **ahead** of another person is in front of them.
-ની આગળ, -ની સામે
*My brother ran **ahead** of us.*

air *noun*
Air is the mixture of gases all around us that we breathe.
હવા
*I opened the window and let in some **air**.*

aircraft *noun*
aircraft
An **aircraft** is any vehicle which can fly.
વિમાન, હવાઈજહાજ

airport *noun*
airports
An **airport** is a place where aeroplanes fly from and land.
વિમાનમથક, હવાઈઅડ્ડો

alarm *noun*
alarms
An **alarm** is a piece of equipment that warns you of danger by making a noise.
ચેતવણા, સૂચના
*The car **alarm** woke us up.*

alien *noun*
aliens
In stories and films, an **alien** is a creature from another planet.
બીજી દુનિયાનું, પરગ્રહી/પરગ્રહવાસી

alike *adjective*
If people or things are **alike**, they are the same in some way.
સરખું, ના જેવું
*The two cats looked **alike**.*

alive *adjective*
If a person, an animal or a plant is **alive**, they are living and not dead.
જીવતું, હયાત

all
You use **all** to talk about everything, everyone, or the whole of something.
તમામ, આખું, સમગ્ર
*Did you eat **all** of it?*

alligator *noun*
alligators
An **alligator** is a large reptile with a long body, a long mouth and sharp teeth. **Alligators'** mouths are in the shape of a letter U.
મગર

allow *verb*
allows, allowing, allowed
If you **allow** someone to do something, you let them do it.
છૂટ કે પરવાનગી આપવી
*Mum **allowed** us to go out and play.*

a
b
c
d
e
f
g
h
i
j
k
l
m
n
o
p
q
r
s
t
u
v
w
x
y
z

A
B
C
D
E
F
G
H
I
J
K
L
M
N
O
P
Q
R
S
T
U
V
W
X
Y
Z

all right or **alright** adjective

If you say that something is **all right**, you mean that it is good enough.
ઠીક
*I thought the film was **all right**.*

almost

Almost means very nearly.
લગભગ, ઘણું કરીને
*I **almost** missed the bus.*

alone adjective

When you are **alone**, you are not with any other people.
એકલું
*She was **alone** in the room.*

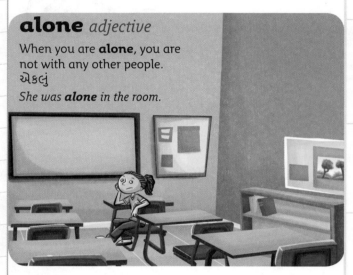

along

1 If you walk **along** a road or other place, you move towards one end of it.
તરફ
*We walked **along** the street.*

2 If you bring something **along** when you go somewhere, you bring it with you.
સાથે
*She brought a present **along** to the party.*

aloud

When you read or talk **aloud**, you read or talk so that other people can hear you.
ઊંચે સાદે, ઘાંટો પાડીને
*She read the story **aloud** to us.*

alphabet noun
alphabets

An **alphabet** is a set of letters that is used for writing words. The letters are arranged in a special order.
વર્ણમાળા, અક્ષરમાળા
*A is the first letter of the **alphabet**.*

already

You use **already** to show that something has happened before the present time.
પહેલેથી, અગાઉથી
*She is **already** here.*

also

You use **also** to give more information about something.
વધુમાં, તદ્ઉપરાંત
*I'm cold, and I'm **also** hungry.*

always

If you **always** do something, you do it every time or all the time.
હંમેશાં
*She's **always** late for school.*

am

⇨ Look at **be**.
*I **am** six years old.*
હોવું

amazing adjective

You say that something is **amazing** when it is a surprise and you like it.
અદ્ભૂત, આશ્ચર્યકારક
*We had an **amazing** holiday.*

ambulance noun
ambulances

An **ambulance** is a vehicle for taking people to hospital.
ઍમ્બ્યુલન્સ, દરદી વાહન

amount noun
amounts

An **amount** of something is how much there is of it.
માત્રા, જથ્થો
*We only have a small **amount** of food.*

amphibian noun
amphibians

An **amphibian** is an animal that lives both on land and in water, for example a frog or a toad.
ઉભયચર(પ્રાણી) જમીન અને પાણી બંનેમાં ચાલનાર

frog

ancient *adjective*

Ancient means very old, or from a long time ago.
પ્રાચીન, પુરાણું, જૂનું
*They lived in an **ancient** castle.*

angry *adjective*
angrier, angriest

When you are **angry**, you feel very upset about something.
ગુસ્સે થયેલું, ક્રૂદ્ધ
*She was **angry** at her brother for breaking the window.*

animal *noun*
animals

An **animal** is any creature that is alive, but not a plant or a person.
પ્રાણી, પશુ

ankle *noun*
ankles

Your **ankle** is the part of your body where your foot joins your leg.
ઘૂંટી
*I fell and twisted my **ankle**.*

annoy *verb*
annoys, annoying, annoyed

If something **annoys** you, it makes you angry and upset.
ગુસ્સે કરવું, સંતાપવું, ચીડવવું
*It **annoys** me when people are rude.*

another

You use **another** to mean one more.
બીજું, વધારાનું
*She ate **another** cake.*

answer *verb*
answers, answering, answered

If you **answer** someone, you say something back to them.
જવાબ કે ઉત્તર આપવો
*She said hello, but he didn't **answer**.*

ant *noun*
ants

Ants are small insects that live in large groups.
કીડી

antelope *noun*
antelopes

An **antelope** is an animal that looks like a deer.
કાળિયાર, હરણ, સાબર

any

1 You use **any** to mean some of a thing.
   જરાક, થોડુંક
   *Is there **any** juice left?*

2 You also use **any** to show that it does not matter which one.
   કોઈ પણ
   *Take **any** book you want.*

anybody

You use **anybody** to talk about a person, when it does not matter which one.
કોઈપણ (માણસ)
*Is there **anybody** there?*

anyone

You use **anyone** to talk about a person, when it does not matter who.
કોઈપણ (માણસ)
*Don't tell **anyone**.*

anything

You use **anything** to talk about a thing, when it does not matter which one.
કાંઈપણ
*I can't see **anything**.*

a
b
c
d
e
f
g
h
i
j
k
l
m
n
o
p
q
r
s
t
u
v
w
x
y
z

anywhere

You use **anywhere** to talk about a place, when it does not matter which one.
ક્યાંય, ગમે ત્યાં
*You can go **anywhere** you like.*

apart

1 When things are **apart**, there is a space or a distance between them.
અલગ અલગ, છેટે
*The desks are too far **apart**.*

2 If you take something **apart**, you take it to pieces.
કકડે કકડા, જુદી જગાએ
*He took his bike **apart**.*

ape *noun*
apes

An **ape** is an animal like a large monkey with long, strong arms and no tail.
પૂંછડા વિનાનો વાંદરો

apologize
or **apologise** *verb*
apologizes, apologizing, apologized

When you **apologize**, you say that you are sorry for something you have said or done.
માફી માગવી, ક્ષમા યાચવી
*He **apologized** for breaking the window.*

appear *verb*
appears, appearing, appeared

When something **appears**, it becomes possible to see it.
દેખાવું
*The sun **appeared** from behind the clouds.*

apple *noun*
apples

An **apple** is a firm, round fruit with green, red, or yellow skin.
સફરજન

April *noun*

April is the month after March and before May. It has 30 days.
એપ્રિલ - વર્ષનો ચોથો મહિનો
*His birthday is in **April**.*

apron *noun*
aprons

An **apron** is a large piece of cloth that you wear over your other clothes to keep them clean when you are cooking or painting.
કપડાં બગડે નહીં તે માટે કપડાંની ઉપર બાંધવાનું ઉપવસ્ત્ર

are

⇨ Look at **be**.
*They **are** both in my class.*

area *noun*
areas

An **area** is a part of a place.
વિસ્તાર, ક્ષેત્ર
*We live in an **area** near the park.*

aren't

Aren't is short for **are not**.
*My friends **aren't** here today.*
નથી

argue *verb*
argues, arguing, argued

If you **argue** with someone, you talk about something that you do not agree about.
દલીલબાજી કરવી
*We **argued** about where to go.*

argument *noun*
arguments

If you have an **argument** with someone, you talk about something that you do not agree about.
દલીલ
*She had an **argument** with another girl.*

arm *noun*
arms

Your **arms** are the two parts of your body between your shoulders and your hands.
ભુજા, બાહુ, હાથ
*She stretched her **arms** out.*

arm

armchair *noun*
armchairs

An **armchair** is a big comfortable chair with parts on the sides for you to put your arms on.
હાથાવાળી આરામખુરશી

army *noun*
armies

An **army** is a large group of soldiers who fight in a war.
સૈન્ય, લશ્કર

around

1 **Around** means in a circle.
આજુબાજુ
*There were lots of people **around** her.*

2 You also use **around** to say that something is in every part of a place.
દરેક બાજુએ, ચોમેર
*His toys lay **around** the room.*

3 **Around** also means near to something.
લગભગ, આશરે
*We left **around** noon.*

arrange *verb*
arranges, arranging, arranged

1 If you **arrange** something, you make plans for it to happen.
ગોઠવવું
*We **arranged** a party for her birthday.*

2 If you **arrange** things somewhere, you put them in a way that looks tidy or pretty.
ગોઠવવું, વ્યવસ્થિત કરવું
*He **arranged** the books in piles.*

arrive *verb*
arrives, arriving, arrived

When you **arrive** at a place, you get there.
આવી પહોંચવું
*We **arrived** ten minutes late.*

arrow *noun*
arrows

1 An **arrow** is a long, thin stick with a sharp point at one end.
તીર, બાણ
*The soldiers used bows and **arrows**.*

2 An **arrow** is also a sign that shows you which way to go.
નિર્દેશક ચિહ્ન
*Follow the **arrows** along the path.*

art *noun*

Art is something that someone has made for people to look at, for example a painting or drawing.
કલા

ask *verb*
asks, asking, asked

1 If you **ask** someone a question, you say that you want to know something.
પૂછવું (સવાલ, માહિતી ઈ.)
*I **asked** him what his name was.*

2 If you **ask** for something, you say that you want it.
કોઈની પાસે માંગવું
*She **asked** for some sweets.*

asleep *adjective*

If you are **asleep**, you are sleeping.
નિદ્રાધીન
*The cat was **asleep** under the tree.*

assembly *noun*
assemblies

An **assembly** is a group of people who meet together.
સભા, બેઠક
*We were late for school **assembly**.*

assistant *noun*
assistants

An **assistant** is someone who helps another person in their work.
મદદનીશ, સહાયક

astronaut *noun*
astronauts

An **astronaut** is a person who travels in space.
અવકાશયાત્રી

a
b
c
d
e
f
g
h
i
j
k
l
m
n
o
p
q
r
s
t
u
v
w
x
y
z

7

A
B
C
D
E
F
G
H
I
J
K
L
M
N
O
P
Q
R
S
T
U
V
W
X
Y
Z

ate
⇒ Look at **eat**.
*He **ate** three apples.*

atlas *noun*
atlases

An **atlas** is a book of maps.
નકશાપોથી

attack *verb*
attacks, attacking, attacked

If someone **attacks** another person, they try to hurt them.
હુમલો કરવો

attention *noun*

If you pay **attention**, you watch and listen.
ધ્યાન, એકાગ્રતા
*He always pays **attention** in class.*

attract *verb*
attracts, attracting, attracted

If something **attracts** things to it, it makes them move towards it.
આકર્ષવું
*Magnets **attract** anything made of iron.*

audience *noun*
audiences

An **audience** is all of the people who watch or listen to something, for example a film or a play.
શ્રોતાજન, પ્રેક્ષક

August *noun*

August is the month after July and before September. It has 31 days.
ઑગસ્ટ - વર્ષનો આઠમો મહિનો
*We went on holiday in **August**.*

aunt *noun*
aunts

Your **aunt** is the sister of your mother or father, or the wife of your uncle.
કાકી, મામી, માશી ફોઈ

author *noun*
authors

An **author** is a person who writes books.
લેખક

autumn *noun*
autumns

Autumn is the season after summer and before winter. In the **autumn** the weather usually becomes cooler and the leaves fall off the trees.
પાનખર, શરદ ઋતુ

awake *adjective*

Someone who is **awake** is not sleeping.
જાગતું,
*I stayed **awake** until midnight.*

away
1 If someone moves **away** from a place, they move so that they are not there any more.
દૂર, આઘે
*He walked **away** from the house.*
2 If you put something **away**, you put it where it should be.
-ની જગ્યાએ
*Put your books **away** before you go.*

awful *adjective*

If something is **awful**, it is very bad.
ખૂબ ખરાબ, ભયંકર
*There was an **awful** smell.*

axe *noun*
axes

An **axe** is a tool with a handle and a big, sharp blade. It is used to chop wood.
કુહાડી

Bb

baby *noun*
babies

A **baby** is a very young child.
શિશુ

back *noun*
backs

1 Your **back** is the part of your body from your neck to your bottom.
પીઠ
*He was lying on his **back** in the grass.*

2 The **back** of something is the side or part of it that is farthest from the front.
પાછળ
*She was in a room at the **back** of the shop.*

backwards

1 If you move **backwards**, you move in the direction behind you.
નીકળ્યા તે તરફ, પાછળ
*She walked **backwards**.*

2 If you do something **backwards**, you do it the opposite of the usual way.
ઊલટી દિશામાં
*He had his jumper on **backwards**.*

bad *adjective*
worse, worst

1 Something that is **bad** is not nice or good.
ખરાબ
*The weather is **bad** today.*

2 Someone who is **bad** does things they should not do.
દુષ્ટ
*Some **bad** boys stole the money.*

badge *noun*
badges

A **badge** is a small piece of metal or plastic with words or a picture on it that you wear on your clothes.
બિલ્લો

badger *noun*
badgers

A **badger** is an animal that has a white head with two black stripes on it. **Badgers** live beneath the ground and come out at night.
એક જાતનું જંગલી પ્રાણી

bag *noun*
bags

A **bag** is a container that you use to hold or carry things.
થેલો, થેલી
*He put his shoes in his **bag**.*

bake *verb*
bakes, baking, baked

When you **bake** food, you cook it in an oven.
શેકવું

baker *noun*
bakers

A **baker** is a person who makes and sells bread and cakes.
બેકરીવાળો

balance *verb*
balances, balancing, balanced

When you **balance** something, you keep it steady and do not let it fall.
સંતુલન
*She **balanced** a book on her head.*

ball *noun*
balls

A **ball** is a round thing that you kick, throw or catch in games.
દડો

ballet *noun*

Ballet is a kind of dance with special steps that often tells a story.
બેલે કરનાર વ્યક્તિઓનો સમૂહ

balloon *noun*
balloons

A **balloon** is a small bag made of thin rubber that you blow into to make it bigger.
ફુગ્ગો

banana *noun*
bananas

A **banana** is a long curved fruit with a thick yellow skin.
કેળું

band *noun*
bands

1 A **band** is a group of people who play music together.
જૂથ, વાજાંવાળાઓની
*He plays the guitar in a **band**.*

2 A **band** is also a narrow strip of material that you put around something.
પટ્ટો, પાટો
*She wore a **band** round her hair.*

bandage *noun*
bandages

A **bandage** is a long strip of cloth that you wrap around a part of your body when you have hurt it.
જખમ ઈ. પર બાંધવાનોપાટો

bang *noun*
bangs

A **bang** is a sudden, loud noise.
ધડાકો
*The balloon burst with a **bang**.*

bank *noun*
banks

1 A **bank** is a place where people can keep their money.
બૅંક, શરાફી પેઢી
*He got some money from the **bank**.*

2 A **bank** is also the ground beside a river.
કિનારો, નદી ઈ.નો કાંઠો
*We walked along the **bank**.*

bar *noun*
bars

A **bar** is a long, thin piece of wood or metal.
સળિયો
*There were **bars** on the windows.*

bare *adjective*
barer, barest

1 If a part of your body is **bare**, it is not covered by any clothes.
ખુલ્લુ, ઉઘાડું
*Her feet were **bare**.*

2 If something is **bare**, it has nothing on top of it or inside it.
ખાલી
*The cupboard was **bare**.*

bark *verb*
barks, barking, barked

When a dog **barks**, it makes a short, loud noise.
ભસવું, ઘરકવું

barn *noun*
barns

A **barn** is a big building on a farm where animals and crops are kept.
ખેતરમાં પાક કે પ્રાણીઓનું ખાણું રાખવાની જગ્યા

base *noun*
bases

The **base** of something is the lowest part of it, or the part that it stands on.
પાયો, આધાર
*She stood at the **base** of the stairs.*

basket *noun*
baskets

A **basket** is a container that you use to hold or carry things. It is made from thin strips of material.
ટોપલી, છાબલી

bat *noun*
bats

1 A **bat** is a special stick that you use to hit a ball in some games.
બૅટ

2 A **bat** is also a small animal that looks like a mouse with wings. **Bats** come out to fly at night.
ચામાચીડિયું, વડવાગોલ

bath *noun*
baths

A **bath** is a long container that you fill with water and sit in to wash yourself.
સ્નાન હોજ

bathroom *noun*
bathrooms

A **bathroom** is a room with a bath or shower in it.
નહાવાની ઓરડી, બાથરૂમ

battery *noun*
batteries

A **battery** is a small tube or box for storing electricity. You put **batteries** in things like toys and radios to make them work.
બેટરી

*The clock needs a new **battery**.*

be *verb*
am, is, are, being, was, were, been

1 You use **be** to say what a person or thing is like.
હોવું, થવું
*She **is** very young.*

2 You also use **be** to say that something is there.
હોવું, થવું
*There **is** a tree in the garden.*

beach *noun*
beaches

A **beach** is the land by the edge of the sea. It is covered with sand or stones.
દરિયાકિનારો

bead *noun*
beads

A **bead** is a small piece of glass, wood or plastic with a hole through the middle. You put **beads** on a string to make necklaces or bracelets.
મણકો

beak *noun*
beaks

A bird's **beak** is the hard part of its mouth.
ચાંચ

bean *noun*
beans

A **bean** is the small seed of some plants that you can eat as a vegetable.
દાણા, કઠોળ

bear *noun*
bears

A **bear** is a big, strong animal with thick fur and sharp claws.
રીંછ

beard *noun*
beards

A **beard** is the hair that grows on a man's chin and cheeks.
દાઢી

beat *verb*
beats, beating, beat, beaten

1 If you **beat** something, you keep hitting it.
ફટકા મારવા
*He **beat** the drum with a stick.*

2 If you **beat** someone in a game or a competition, you do better than they do.
હરાવવું
*He **beat** me in the race.*

beautiful
adjective

If something is **beautiful**, it is very nice to look at or to listen to.
સુંદર, મોહક
*He painted a **beautiful** picture.*

became
⇨ Look at **become**.
*She **became** very angry.*

a
b
c
d
e
f
g
h
i
j
k
l
m
n
o
p
q
r
s
t
u
v
w
x
y
z

because

You use **because** to say why something happens.
કારણકે
*I went to bed **because** I was tired.*

become *verb*
becomes, becoming, became, become

If one thing **becomes** another thing, it starts to be that thing.
બનવું, બની જવું
*The weather **became** cold.*

bed *noun*
beds

A **bed** is a piece of furniture that you lie on when you sleep.
પથારી, ખાટલો, પલંગ

bedroom *noun*
bedrooms

A **bedroom** is a room with a bed in it where you sleep.
સૂવાનો ઓરડો, શયન ખંડ

bedtime *noun*
bedtimes

Your **bedtime** is the time when you usually go to bed.
સૂવાનો સમય
*My **bedtime** is at eight o'clock.*

bee *noun*
bees

A **bee** is an insect with wings and black and yellow stripes on its body.
Bees live in large groups and make honey.
મધમાખી

been

⇨ Look at **be**.
*We have always **been** good friends.*

beetle *noun*
beetles

A **beetle** is an insect with hard wings that cover its body when it is not flying.
વાંદો, એક જાતનો જીવડો

before

If one thing happens **before** another thing, it happens earlier than it.
પૂર્વે, અગાઉ
*My birthday is just **before** his.*

began

⇨ Look at **begin**.
*She **began** to laugh.*

begin *verb*
begins, beginning, began, begun

If you **begin** to do something, you start to do it.
શરૂ કરવું
*You can **begin** to write now.*

begun

⇨ Look at **begin**.
*He has **begun** to play the piano.*

behave *verb*
behaves, behaving, behaved

1   The way you **behave** is the way that you do and say things.
વર્તન કરવું
*She **behaves** like a baby.*

2   If you **behave** yourself, you are good.
સારી રીતભાત
*You can come if you **behave** yourself.*

behind

If something is **behind** another thing, it is at the back of it.
પાછળ
*He stood **behind** his desk.*

believe *verb*
believes, believing, believed

If you **believe** something, you think that it is true.
માનવું
*I don't **believe** that story.*

bell *noun*
bells

A **bell** is a piece of metal in the shape of a cup that rings when you shake it or hit it.
ઘંટડી, ઘંટ

belong *verb*
belongs, belonging, belonged

1 If something **belongs** to you, it is yours.
ની માલિકીનું
*The book **belongs** to her.*

2 If you **belong** to a group of people, you are one of them.
સભ્ય હોવું, જોડાયેલું હોવું
*He **belongs** to our team.*

3 If something **belongs** somewhere, that is where it should be.
યોગ્ય રીતે મુકાયેલું હોવું
*Your toys **belong** in your room.*

below

If something is **below** another thing, it is lower down than it.
નીચે
*His shoes were **below** his bed.*

belt *noun*
belts

A **belt** is a band of leather or cloth that you wear around your waist.
કમર પર પહેરવાનો ચામડાનો કે કપડાનો પટ્ટો

bench *noun*
benches

A **bench** is a long seat that two or more people can sit on.
બાંકડો

bend *verb*
bends, bending, bent

When you **bend** something, you change its shape so that it is not straight any more.
વાળવું
***Bend** your legs when you do this exercise.*

beneath

If something is **beneath** another thing, it is below it.
નીચે
*The dog was **beneath** the table.*

bent

⇨ Look at **bend**.
*He **bent** to pick up the bags.*

berry *noun*
berries

A **berry** is a small, soft fruit that grows on a bush or a tree.
બોર

beside

If something is **beside** another thing, it is next to it.
બાજુમાં
*He sat down **beside** me.*

best

If you say that something is **best**, you mean that it is better than all the others.
ઉત્તમ, શ્રેષ્ઠ
*You are my **best** friend.*

a
b
c
d
e
f
g
h
i
j
k
l
m
n
o
p
q
r
s
t
u
v
w
x
y
z

better

1 You use **better** to mean that a thing is very good compared to another thing.
વધારે સારું
*His painting is **better** than mine.*

2 If you feel **better**, you do not feel ill any more.
બહેતર,
*I feel much **better** today.*

between

If you are **between** two things, one of them is on one side of you and the other is on the other side.
વચ્ચે
*She stood **between** her two brothers.*

bicycle *noun*
bicycles

A **bicycle** is a vehicle with two wheels. You push the pedals with your feet to make the wheels turn.
સાયકલ

big *adjective*
bigger, biggest

A person or thing that is **big** is large in size.
મોટું
*She lives in a **big** house.*

bike *noun*
bikes

A **bike** is a bicycle or motorbike.
બાઈસિકલ

bin *noun*
bins

A **bin** is a container that you put rubbish in.
કચરાપેટી

bird *noun*
birds

A **bird** is an animal with feathers, wings, and a beak. Most **birds** can fly.
પક્ષી

birthday *noun*
birthdays

Your **birthday** is the date that you were born.
જન્મદિવસ
*She gave me a present on my **birthday**.*

biscuit *noun*
biscuits

A **biscuit** is a kind of small, hard, dry cake.
બિસ્કીટ

bit *noun*
bits

A **bit** of something is a small amount of it, or a small part of it.
નાનો ટુકડો, હિસ્સો
*I ate a **bit** of bread.*

bite *verb*
bites, biting, bit, bitten

If you **bite** something, you use your teeth to cut into it.
કરડવું, બચકું ભરવું
*The dog tried to **bite** him.*

black *noun*

Black is the colour of the sky at night.
કાળુ
*The car is **black**.*

blackboard *noun*
blackboards

A **blackboard** is a flat, black surface that you write on with chalk in a classroom.
બોર્ડ, લખવાનું પાટિયું

blade *noun*
blades

A **blade** is the flat, sharp part of a knife that you use to cut things.
ધારદાર પતરી

blame verb
blames, blaming, blamed
If you **blame** someone for something bad, you think that they made it happen.
દોષ કાઢવો
*Mum **blamed** me for making the mess.*

blanket noun
blankets
A **blanket** is a large, thick piece of cloth that you put on a bed to keep you warm.
ધાબળી

blew
⇨ Look at **blow**.
*The wind **blew** outside.*

blind adjective
Someone who is **blind** cannot see.
આંધળુ, દૃષ્ટિહીન

block noun
blocks
A **block** of something is a large piece of it with straight sides.
શિલા, બ્લોક
*We made a house with **blocks** of wood.*

blood noun
Blood is the red liquid that moves around inside your body.
રક્ત, રુધિર, લોહી

blouse noun
blouses
A **blouse** is something a girl or woman can wear. It covers the top part of the body and has buttons down the front.
સ્ત્રીઓ માટેની ચોળી, બ્લાઉઝ

blow verb
blows, blowing, blew, blown
1 When the wind **blows**, it moves the air.
ફૂંકાવું, વાવું (પવન,હવા અંગે)
2 When you **blow**, you push air out of your mouth.
ફૂંક મારવી
*He **blew** on his hands to keep them warm.*

blue noun
Blue is the colour of the sky on a sunny day.
વાદળી, આસમાની
*Her dress is **blue**.*

blunt adjective
blunter, bluntest
Something that is **blunt** does not have a sharp point or edge.
બુઠું, અણી વિનાનું
*My pencil is **blunt**.*

boat noun
boats
A **boat** is a small vehicle that carries people on water.
હોડી

body noun
bodies
A person's or animal's **body** is all their parts.
શરીર
*It's fun to stretch and twist your **body**.*

boil verb
boils, boiling, boiled
1 When water **boils**, it becomes very hot, and you can see bubbles in it and steam coming from it.
ઉકળવું, ઉકાળવું
2 When you **boil** food, you cook it in water that is boiling.
બાફવું,

bone noun
bones
Your **bones** are the hard parts inside your body.
હાડકું, અસ્થિ
*I broke a **bone** in my leg.*

A
B
C
D
E
F
G
H
I
J
K
L
M
N
O
P
Q
R
S
T
U
V
W
X
Y
Z

bonfire *noun*
bonfires

A **bonfire** is a big fire that is made outside.
કચરો બાળવાની અગ્નિ

book *noun*
books

A **book** is a set of pages with words or pictures on them, that are held together inside a cover.
પુસ્તક

boot *noun*
boots

A **boot** is a kind of shoe that covers your foot and the lower part of your leg.
બૂટ, જોડો

bored *adjective*

If you are **bored**, you feel annoyed because you have nothing to do.
કંટાળેલું

boring *adjective*

If something is **boring**, it is not interesting.
કંટાળાજનક

born *verb*

When a baby is **born**, it comes out of its mother's body.
જન્મવું, પેદા થવું
*My sister was **born** three years ago.*

borrow *verb*
borrows, borrowing, borrowed

If you **borrow** something from someone, they let you have it for a short time and then you give it back.
ઉછીનું લેવું
*Can I **borrow** your pen, please?*

both

You use **both** to mean two people or two things together.
બંને
*He put **both** books into the drawer.*

bottle *noun*
bottles

A **bottle** is a container made of glass or plastic that holds liquid.
શીશી

bottom *noun*
bottoms

1   The **bottom** of something is its lowest part.
તદ્દન નીચેનો ભાગ, તળિયું

2   Your **bottom** is the part of your body that you sit on.
કૂલા,

bought

⇨ Look at **buy**.
*We **bought** bread and milk.*

bounce *verb*
bounces, bouncing, bounced

When something **bounces**, it hits another thing and then moves away from it again.
ઉછળવું
*The ball **bounced** across the floor.*

bow *verb*
bows, bowing, bowed

When you **bow**, you bend your body towards someone as a polite way of saying hello or thanking them.
નમવું, નમસ્કાર કરવા
*They all **bowed** to the king.*

bow *noun*
bows

1   A **bow** is a knot with two loose ends that you use to tie laces and ribbons.
એક કે બે ગાળાવાળી

2   A **bow** is also a long, curved piece of wood with a string stretched between the two ends, that is used to send arrows through the air.
કામઠું

bowl noun
bowls

A **bowl** is a round container that you use to hold food or drink.
વાડકો

box noun
boxes

A **box** is a container with a hard, straight bottom and sides, and usually a lid.
ખાનું

boy noun
boys

A **boy** is a male child.
છોકરો

bracelet noun
bracelets

A **bracelet** is a chain or a band that you wear around your wrist.
હાથમાં પહેરવાનું ઘરેણું

brain noun
brains

Your **brain** is inside your head. It controls your body and lets you think and feel things.
દિમાગ, મગજ

branch noun
branches

The **branches** of a tree are the parts that grow out from its trunk and have leaves on them.
શાખા, ડાળી

brave adjective
braver, bravest

If you are **brave**, you are not afraid of something dangerous.
બહાદુર, શૌર્યવાન, વીર

bread noun

Bread is a food that is made from flour and water and baked in an oven.
બ્રેડ

break verb
breaks, breaking, broke, broken

1 When something **breaks**, it goes into pieces.
તૂટવું, ફૂટવું
I dropped a plate and it broke.

2 When a machine **breaks**, it stops working.
ભાંગવું, ફ્રેડવું, તોડવું
My brother broke the television.

breakfast noun
breakfasts

Breakfast is the first meal of the day.
સવારનો નાસ્તો

breathe verb
breathes, breathing, breathed

When you **breathe**, air goes in and out of your body through your nose or your mouth.
શ્વાસ લેવો

brick noun
bricks

Bricks are small blocks of baked earth used for building.
ઈંટ

bride noun
brides

A **bride** is a woman who is getting married.
નવવધુ, નવોઢા

bridegroom *noun*
bridegrooms
A **bridegroom** is a man who is getting married.
વરરાજા

bridge *noun*
bridges
A **bridge** is something that is built over a river, a road, or a railway so that people can get across it.
પુલ, સેતુ

bright *adjective*
brighter, brightest
1 A **bright** colour is very easy to see.
ઉઠાવદાર, ભભકાવાળું
*She wore a **bright** red dress.*

2 Something that is **bright** shines with a lot of light.
તેજસ્વી
*The sun is very **bright** today.*

brilliant *adjective*
Something that is **brilliant** is very good.
ખૂબ બુદ્ધિશાળી
*I thought the film was **brilliant**.*

bring *verb*
brings, bringing, brought
If you **bring** something, you take it with you when you go somewhere.
લાવવું, લઈ આવવું
*You can **bring** a friend to the party.*

broke
⇨ Look at **break**.
*I'm sorry I **broke** the radio.*

broken *adjective*
If something is **broken**, it is in pieces.
ભાંગેલું, તૂટેલું, ફૂટેલું
*All of his toys are **broken**.*

broom *noun*
brooms
A **broom** is a brush with a long handle that you use to sweep the floor.
સાવરણી, ઝાડુ

brother *noun*
brothers
Your **brother** is a boy or a man who has the same mother and father as you do.
સગો ભાઈ, સહોદર

brought
⇨ Look at **bring**.
*We **brought** some food for the picnic.*

brown *noun*
Brown is the colour of earth or wood.
તપખીરી બદામી
*Her eyes are dark **brown**.*

bruise *noun*
bruises
A **bruise** is a purple mark on your skin that appears if something hits a part of your body.
ચકામું
*She has a big **bruise** on her leg.*

brush *noun*
brushes
A **brush** has lots of short hairs fixed to a handle. You use a **brush** to make your hair tidy, to clean things, or to paint.
પીંછી કરવાનું બ્રશ

A B C D E F G H I J K L M N O P Q R S T U V W X Y Z

bubble *noun*
bubbles

A **bubble** is a small ball of liquid with air inside it.
પરપોટો

bucket *noun*
buckets

A **bucket** is a deep, round container with a handle that you use to hold or carry liquids.
બાલટી, ડોલ

buckle *noun*
buckles

A **buckle** is something you use to fasten a belt, a shoe or a bag.
કડી, બકલ

bud *noun*
buds

A **bud** is a small, new part on a tree or plant that grows into a leaf or a flower.
અંકુર, ફણગો

build *verb*
builds, building, built

If you **build** something, you make it by putting the parts of it together.
ચણવું, બાંધવું, નિર્માણ કરવું
*They are going to **build** the school here.*

building *noun*
buildings

A **building** is a place with walls and a roof.
મકાન, ઈમારત
*Houses, shops and schools are all **buildings**.*

built

⇨ Look at **build**.
*We **built** our house on a hill.*

bulb *noun*
bulbs

A **bulb** is the part of a lamp that is made of glass and gives out light.
પોટો, બલ્બ

bull *noun*
bulls

A **bull** is a male cow. **Bulls** have horns.
બળદ

bump *verb*
bumps, bumping, bumped

If you **bump** something, or **bump** into it, you hit it without meaning to.
અચાનક ભટકાઈ જવું, અચાનક ટક્કર
*I **bumped** the table with my bag.*

bunch *noun*
bunches

A **bunch** of things is a group of them.
ઝૂમખું, ગુચ્છો
*He held a **bunch** of keys.*

bundle *noun*
bundles

A **bundle** is a lot of clothes, sticks or other things that are fastened together.
(કપડાનું) પોટલું, ભારી

buried

⇨ Look at **bury**.
*The pirates **buried** the gold beneath a tree.*

burn *verb*
burns, burning, burned, burnt

1 If you **burn** something, you destroy it or damage it with fire.
બાળવું
*He **burned** all the rubbish.*

2 If you **burn** yourself, you touch something that is hot and get hurt.
દાઝવું
*I **burned** myself on the hot iron.*

3 If something is **burning**, it is on fire.
આગ લાગવી
*The bonfire is still **burning**.*

A
B
C
D
E
F
G
H
I
J
K
L
M
N
O
P
Q
R
S
T
U
V
W
X
Y
Z

burst *verb*
bursts, bursting, burst

When something **bursts**, it breaks open suddenly.
ફાટવું, વિસ્ફોટ થવો
*The bag **burst** and everything fell out of it.*

bury *verb*
buries, burying, buried

If you **bury** something, you put it into a hole in the ground and cover it up.
દાટવું, દફનાવવું
*Squirrels **bury** nuts to eat in the winter.*

bus *noun*
buses

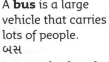

A **bus** is a large vehicle that carries lots of people.
બસ
*I go to school on the **bus**.*

bush *noun*
bushes

A **bush** is a plant with lots of leaves and branches that is smaller than a tree.
નાનું ઝાડ, ઝાડવું

busy *adjective*
busier, busiest

1 If you are **busy**, you have a lot of things to do.
પ્રવૃત્ત, પૂરેપૂરું
*We were **busy** cleaning the house.*

2 A **busy** place is full of people.
ધમાલિયું
*The shops are **busy** today.*

butcher *noun*
butchers

A **butcher** is a person who sells meat.
કસાઈ

butter *noun*

Butter is a soft yellow and white food that is made from cream. You spread it on bread or cook with it.
માખણ

butterfly *noun*
butterflies

A **butterfly** is an insect with four large wings.
પતંગિયું

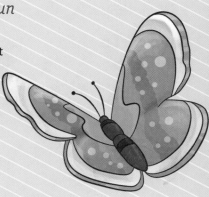

button *noun*
buttons

Buttons are small, round things on clothes that you push through holes to fasten the clothes together.
બટન

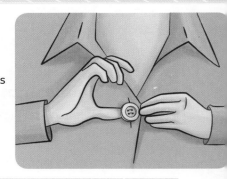

buy *verb*
buys, buying, bought

If you **buy** something, you pay money so that you can have it.
ખરીદવું
*We went into the shop to **buy** sweets.*

buzz *verb*
buzzes, buzzing, buzzed

If something **buzzes**, it makes a sound like a bee makes when it flies.
ગણગણાટ કરવો
*An insect **buzzed** around my head.*

Cc

cabbage *noun*
cabbages

A **cabbage** is a round vegetable with green, white, or purple leaves.
કોબી (શાક)

cage *noun*
cages

A **cage** is a box or a room made of bars where you keep birds or animals.
પાંજરું

cake *noun*
cakes

A **cake** is a sweet food made from flour, eggs, sugar, and butter that you bake in an oven.
કેક

calculator *noun*
calculators

A **calculator** is a small machine that you use to do sums.
ગણકયંત્ર

calendar *noun*
calendars

A **calendar** is a list of all the days, weeks, and months in a year.
પંચાંગ, કૅલેન્ડર

calf *noun*
calves

1 A **calf** is a young cow.
વાછરડું
2 Your **calves** are also the thick parts at the backs of your legs, between your ankles and your knees.
પગની પિંડી, ગોટલો

call *verb*
calls, calling, called

1 If you **call** someone something, you give them a name.
નામ પાડવું
*I **called** my cat Pippin.*

2 If you **call** something, you say it in a loud voice.
બૂમ પાડવી, હાક મારવી
*Someone **called** his name.*

3 If you **call** someone, you talk to them on the telephone.
ટેલિફોનથી સંપર્ક
*I'll **call** you tomorrow.*

calves

⇨ Look at **calf**.
*My **calves** hurt.*

came

⇨ Look at **come**.
*My friends **came** to play at my house.*

camel *noun*
camels

A **camel** is a large animal with one or two big lumps on its back. **Camels** live in hot, dry places and carry people and things.
ઊંટ

camera *noun*
cameras

A **camera** is a machine that you use to take pictures.
કૅમેરા

camp *noun*
camps

A **camp** is a place where people live in tents for a short time.
છાવણી, પડાવ

can *verb*
could

If you **can** do something, you are able to do it.
કરી શકવું
*I **can** swim.*

a b c d e f g h i j k l m n o p q r s t u v w x y z

A
B
C
D
E
F
G
H
I
J
K
L
M
N
O
P
Q
R
S
T
U
V
W
X
Y
Z

can *noun*
cans

A **can** is a metal container for food or drink.
પતરાનો ડબો

*She opened a **can** of soup.*

candle *noun*
candles

A **candle** is a stick of wax with a piece of string through the middle that you burn to give you light.
મીણબત્તી

cannot *verb*

If you **cannot** do something, you are not able to do it.
ન કરી શકવું

*I **cannot** find my bag.*

can't

Can't is short for **cannot**.

*He **can't** play the piano.*

capital *noun*
capitals

1   The **capital** of a country is the main city, where the country's leaders work.
રાજધાની

*Paris is the **capital** of France.*

2   A **capital** is also a big letter of the alphabet, for example A or R.
મોટો (કૅપિટલ)

car *noun*
cars

A **car** is a vehicle with four wheels and an engine that can carry a small number of people.
ગાડી -મોટરગાડી

card *noun*
cards

1   **Card** is stiff paper.
જાડો કે પૂંઠાનો કાગળ

2   A **card** is a folded piece of stiff paper that has a picture on the front and a message inside. You send **cards** to people at special times, like birthdays.
આમંત્રણપત્રિકા

3   **Cards** are pieces of stiff paper with numbers or pictures on them that you use for playing games.
ગંજીફાનું પત્તું, પત્તાં (રમવાં તે),

cardboard *noun*

Cardboard is very thick, stiff paper that is used for making boxes.
પૂઠું

care *verb*
cares, caring, cared

1   If you **care** about something, you think that it is important.
પરવા કરવી, ચિંતા કરવી

*He doesn't **care** about the way he looks.*

2   If you **care** for a person or an animal, you look after them.
કાળજી, દેખરેખ

*She **cared** for her pets.*

careful *adjective*

If you are **careful**, you think about what you are doing so that you do not make any mistakes.
સાવચેત, સાવધાન, ખબરદાર

*Be **careful** when you cross the road.*

careless *adjective*

If you are **careless**, you do not think about what you are doing, so that you make mistakes.
બેદરકાર

*It was **careless** of me to forget my keys.*

carpet *noun*
carpets

A **carpet** is a thick, soft cover for a floor.
જાજમ

carpet

carrot *noun*
carrots

A **carrot** is a long, orange vegetable.
ગાજર

carry *verb*
carries, carrying, carried

If you **carry** something, you hold it and take it somewhere with you.
ઉપાડીને લઇ જવું

*We **carried** our bags to the car.*

carton *noun*
cartons

A **carton** is a container made of plastic or cardboard that is used to hold food or drink.
પૂઠાનું ખોખું, પેટી કે ડબ્બો
*I bought a **carton** of milk.*

cartoon *noun*
cartoons

1 A **cartoon** is a funny drawing.
વ્યંગ્યચિત્ર, હાસ્યચિત્ર

2 A **cartoon** is also a film that uses drawings, not real people or things.
વ્યંગ ચિત્રોના ફોટા લઈને તે પરથી બનાવેલો ફોટો

case *noun*
cases

A **case** is a container that is used to hold or carry something.
ખોખું, પેટી
*He put the camera in its **case**.*

castle *noun*
castles

A **castle** is a large building with very thick, high walls. Most **castles** were built a long time ago to keep the people inside safe from their enemies.
કિલ્લો

cat *noun*
cats

A **cat** is an animal that is covered with fur and has a long tail. People often keep small **cats** as pets. Large **cats**, for example lions and tigers, are wild.
બિલાડી, બિલાડો

catch *verb*
catches, catching, caught

1 If you **catch** something that is moving, you take hold of it while it is in the air.
પકડવું, ઝીલવું, ઝાલવું
*I tried to **catch** the ball.*

2 If you **catch** a bus or a train, you get on it.
ગાડી, બસ, ઇ.
*We **caught** the bus to school.*

3 If you **catch** an illness, you become ill with it.
નો ચેપ

*He **caught** measles.*

caterpillar *noun*
caterpillars

A **caterpillar** is a small animal that looks like a worm with lots of short legs. **Caterpillars** turn into butterflies or moths.
ઈયળ

cattle *noun*

Cattle are cows and bulls.
ઢોર
*There were **cattle** in the field.*

caught

⇨ Look at **catch**.
*I jumped and **caught** the ball.*

cauliflower *noun*
cauliflowers

A **cauliflower** is a big, round, white vegetable with green leaves.
ફૂલકોબી

cave *noun*
caves

A **cave** is a big hole in the side of a hill or a mountain, or beneath the ground.
ગુફા

CD *noun*
CDs

CD is short for compact disc.
સીડી
*I bought the band's new **CD**.*

A
B
C
D
E
F
G
H
I
J
K
L
M
N
O
P
Q
R
S
T
U
V
W
X
Y
Z

ceiling *noun*
ceilings

A **ceiling** is the part of a room that is above your head.
છત

centimetre *noun*
centimetres

A **centimetre** is used for measuring the length of something. There are ten millimetres in a **centimetre**, and one hundred **centimetres** in a metre.
મીટરનો સોમો ભાગ

centre *noun*
centres

The **centre** of something is the middle of it.
મધ્યબિંદુ

*She stood in the **centre** of the room.*

cereal *noun*
cereals

1 A **cereal** is a food made from grains that you eat with milk for breakfast.
એક પ્રકારનો નાસ્તો

2 A **cereal** is also a kind of plant, for example wheat or rice. The seeds of **cereals** are used for food.
(એકદલ) અનાજ કે તેનો છોડ

chain *noun*
chains

A **chain** is a row of rings made of metal that are joined together in a line.
સાંકળ

chair *noun*
chairs

A **chair** is a seat with a back and four legs, for one person.
ખુરશી

*He suddenly got up from his **chair**.*

chalk *noun*

Chalk is a kind of soft rock. You use small sticks of **chalk** to write or draw on a blackboard.
ચાક, ખડી,

change *verb*
changes, changing, changed

1 When you **change** something, or when it **changes**, it becomes different.

*The caterpillar **changed** into a butterfly.*

2 When you **change**, you put on different clothes.
બદલવું કે બદલાવું,ફેરફાર કરવો કે થવો
*He **changed** to go to the party.*

change *noun*

Change is the money that you get back when you pay too much for something.
પરચૂરણ

chapter *noun*
chapters

A **chapter** is a part of a book.
પુસ્તકનું પ્રકરણ, અધ્યાય
*This book has ten **chapters**.*

character *noun*
characters

1 Your **character** is the kind of person you are.
વ્યક્તિત્વ,

2 A **character** is also a person in a story or a film.
નાટક,નવલકથા, ઇ.નું પાત્ર

charge *verb*
charges, charging, charged

If someone **charges** you an amount of money for something, they ask you to pay that amount for it.
-ની કિંમત માગવી
*They **charged** us too much for our meal.*

chase *verb*
chases, chasing, chased

If you **chase** someone, you run after them and try to catch them.
પીછો કરવો
*The dog **chased** the cat.*

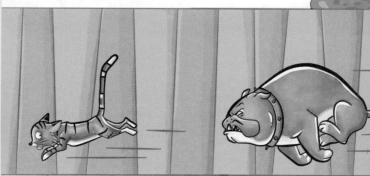

cheap *adjective*
cheaper, cheapest

If something is **cheap**, you do not have to pay a lot of money for it.
સસ્તું

*Milk is very **cheap** in this shop.*

check *verb*
checks, checking, checked

If you **check** something, you make sure that it is right.
તપાસવું

*The teacher **checked** my homework.*

cheek *noun*
cheeks

Your **cheeks** are the sides of your face below your eyes.
ગાલ

*My **cheeks** were red.*

cheer *verb*
cheers, cheering, cheered

When people **cheer**, they shout to show that they like something.
હર્ષનાદ:

*We all **cheered** when he won the race.*

cheerful *adjective*

Someone who is **cheerful** is happy.
ખુશમિજાજ

cheese *noun*

Cheese is a solid food that is made from milk.
ચીઝ

cheetah *noun*
cheetahs

A **cheetah** is a big wild cat with yellow fur and black spots.
ચિત્તો

cherry *noun*
cherries

A **cherry** is a small, round fruit with a hard stone in the middle. **Cherries** are red, black, or yellow.
ઠળિયાવાળું એક નાનું ફળ

chew *verb*
chews, chewing, chewed

When you **chew** food, you use your teeth to break it up in your mouth before you swallow it.
ચાવવું

chick *noun*
chicks

A **chick** is a very young bird.
ઈંડું સેવાય તે પહેલાંનું કે ત્યાર પછીનું પક્ષીનું બચ્ચું

chicken *noun*
chickens

1   A **chicken** is a bird that is kept on a farm for its eggs and meat.
પાળેલું મરઘું,

2   **Chicken** is also the meat that comes from chickens.
મરઘાનું માંસ,

child *noun*
children

A **child** is a young boy or girl.
બાળક

chimney *noun*
chimneys

A **chimney** is a long pipe above a fire. Smoke from the fire goes up the **chimney** and out of the building.
ધુમાડિયું

chimpanzee *noun*
chimpanzees

A **chimpanzee** is a kind of small ape with dark fur.
માનવસદૃશ વાનર

a
b
c
d
e
f
g
h
i
j
k
l
m
n
o
p
q
r
s
t
u
v
w
x
y
z

A
B
C
D
E
F
G
H
I
J
K
L
M
N
O
P
Q
R
S
T
U
V
W
X
Y
Z

chin noun
chins

Your **chin** is the part of your face below your mouth.
હડપચી
A black beard covered his **chin**.

chip noun
chips

Chips or potato **chips** are thin pieces of potato fried in hot oil.
બટાટાની કાતરી

chip verb
chips, chipping, chipped

If you **chip** something, you break a small piece off it by accident.
ચીપ કે છોડું ઉતરવું
I **chipped** *my tooth when I fell.*

chocolate noun
chocolates

Chocolate is a sweet brown food that is used to make sweets, cakes, and drinks.
ચોકલેટ

choose verb
chooses, choosing, chose, chosen

If you **choose** something, you decide to have it.
પસંદ કરવું
You can **choose** *any book you want.*

chop verb
chops, chopping, chopped

If you **chop** something, you cut it into pieces with a knife or an axe.
કાપવું
He **chopped** *some wood for the fire.*

chose
➡ Look at **choose**.
She **chose** *a dress to wear.*

chosen
➡ Look at **choose**.
We have **chosen** *which film to watch.*

circle noun
circles

A **circle** is a round shape.
વર્તુળ, કુંડાળું

circus noun
circuses

A **circus** is a big tent where you go to see clowns and animals.
સરકસ

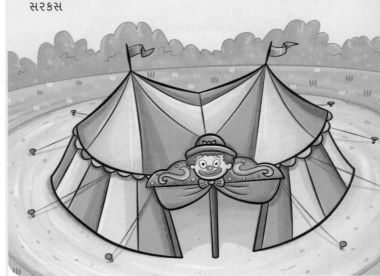

city noun
cities

A **city** is a very big town where a lot of people live and work.
શહેર

clap verb
claps, clapping, clapped

When you **clap**, you hit your hands together to make a loud noise. People **clap** to show that they like something.
તાળી પાડવી
Everyone **clapped** *at the end of her song.*

class noun
classes

A **class** is a group of people who are taught together.
વર્ગ અથવા શ્રેણી
He is in my **class** *at school.*

classroom *noun*
classrooms

A **classroom** is a room in a school where children have lessons.
વર્ગખંડ

claw *noun*
claws

A bird's or an animal's **claws** are the hard, sharp, curved parts at the end of its feet.
પશુ કે પંખીના નહોર

clean *adjective*
cleaner, cleanest

Something that is **clean** does not have any dirt or marks on it.
સ્વચ્છ
*Make sure your hands are **clean**.*

clean *verb*
cleans, cleaning, cleaned

When you **clean** something, you take all the dirt off it.
સાફ કરવું
*I **clean** my teeth before bedtime.*

clear *adjective*
clearer, clearest

1 If something is **clear**, it is easy to understand, to see, or to hear.
સ્પષ્ટ, ચોખ્ખું
*He gave us **clear** instructions on what to do.*

2 If something like glass or plastic is **clear**, you can see through it.
સ્વચ્છ
*The bottle was full of a **clear** liquid.*

3 If a place is **clear**, it does not have anything there that you do not want.
ખુલ્લું, મોકળું
*You can cross the road when it is **clear**.*

clear *verb*
clears, clearing, cleared

When you **clear** a place, you take away all the things you do not want there.
સાફ કરવું
*She **cleared** the table.*

clever *adjective*
cleverer, cleverest

Someone who is **clever** can learn and understand things quickly.
હોશિયાર
*She is very **clever** at maths.*

cliff *noun*
cliffs

A **cliff** is a hill with one side that is very steep. **Cliffs** are often beside the sea.
સીધો-ઊભો ખડક

climb *verb*
climbs, climbing, climbed

If you **climb** something, you move towards the top of it. You sometimes use your hands as well as your feet when you **climb**.
ઉપર જવું, ચડવું
*We **climbed** the tree in the garden.*

cloak *noun*
cloaks

A **cloak** is a very loose coat without sleeves.
ઢીલો ડગલો

clock *noun*
clocks

A **clock** is a machine that shows you the time.
ઘડિયાળ

close *verb*
closes, closing, closed

When you **close** something, you shut it.
બંધ કરવું કે થવું
*Please **close** the door behind you.*

a b c d e f g h i j k l m n o p q r s t u v w x y z

A
B
C
D
E
F
G
H
I
J
K
L
M
N
O
P
Q
R
S
T
U
V
W
X
Y
Z

close *adjective*
closer, closest

If something is **close** to another thing, it is near it.
નજીક, અડીને, પાસેપાસે
Our house is close to the park.

cloth *noun*
cloths

1 **Cloth** is material that is used to make things like clothes and curtains.
કાપડ

2 A **cloth** is a piece of material that you use to clean something.
કપડું

clothes *noun*

Clothes are the things that people wear, for example shirts, trousers, and dresses.
કપડાં, વસ્ત્રો

cloud *noun*
clouds

A **cloud** is a white or grey shape that you see in the sky. **Clouds** are made of tiny drops of water that sometimes turn into rain.
વાદળું

clown *noun*
clowns

A **clown** is a person who wears funny clothes and does silly things to make people laugh.
મૂક નાટક કે સરકસમાં વિદૂષક

coat *noun*
coats

You wear a **coat** on top of your other clothes when you go outside.
કોટ, ડગલો

cobweb *noun*
cobwebs

A **cobweb** is a very thin net that a spider makes to catch insects.
કરોળિયાનું જાળું

coconut *noun*
coconuts

A **coconut** is a very large nut that has a very hard shell and is white inside. **Coconuts** are full of a liquid called **coconut** milk.
નાળિયેર

coffee *noun*

Coffee is a drink. You make it by pouring hot water on **coffee** beans.
કૉફી
Coffee beans grow on a coffee plant.

coin *noun*
coins

A **coin** is a round, flat piece of metal that is used as money.
ચલણી સિક્કો

cold *adjective*
colder, coldest

1 If you are **cold**, you do not feel comfortable because you are not warm enough.
ટાઢું લાગતું
Wear a jumper if you are cold.

2 If something is **cold**, it is not hot.
ઠંડું
The weather is very cold.

cold *noun*
colds

When you have a **cold**, you sneeze and cough a lot, and you have a sore throat.
શરદી

collar *noun*
collars

1 The **collar** of a shirt or jacket is the part that goes around your neck.
ગળાપટ્ટી

2 A **collar** is also a band that goes around the neck of a dog or cat.
જાનવરને ગળે બંધાતો પટ્ટો

collect *verb*
collects, collecting, collected

1 If you **collect** things, you bring them together.
   ભેગું કરવું, એકત્ર કરવું
   *He **collected** wood for the fire.*

2 If you **collect** someone from a place, you go there and take them away.
   આણવું કે લાવવું
   *Mum **collected** us from school.*

colour *noun*
colours

Red, blue and yellow are the main **colours**. You can mix them together to make other **colours**.
રંગ, વર્ણ, કોઈ ખાસ રંગ

comb *noun*
combs

A **comb** is a flat piece of metal or plastic with very thin points that you use to make your hair tidy.
દાંતિયો, કાંસકો

come *verb*
comes, coming, came, come

When you **come** to a place, you move towards it or arrive there.
આવવું, પાસે આવવું
*She **came** into the room.*

comfortable *adjective*

If something is **comfortable**, it makes you feel good.
તન અને મનથી સુખી સ્વસ્થ, આરામદાયક
*This is a very **comfortable** chair.*

comic *noun*
comics

A **comic** is a magazine with stories that are told in pictures.
ચિત્રવાર્તાવાળું સામયિક

common *adjective*

If things are **common**, you see lots of them around, or they happen often.
બધાનું સહિયારું, વારંવાર થતું, સામાન્ય
*Foxes are quite **common** in this area.*

compact disc *noun*
compact discs

A **compact disc** is a round, flat piece of plastic that has music or information on it. **Compact discs** are also called CDs.
કૉમ્પૅક્ટ ડિસ્ક

competition *noun*
competitions

When you are in a **competition**, you try to show that you are the best at something.
સ્પર્ધા, હરીફાઈ
*She won the painting **competition**.*

complete *adjective*

If something is **complete**, none of it is missing.
સંપૂર્ણ, સમાપ્ત
*He had a **complete** set of crayons.*

computer *noun*
computers

A **computer** is a machine that can store a lot of information and can work things out very quickly.
ગણકયંત્ર, કમ્પ્યૂટર
*We played games on our **computer**.*

confused *adjective*

If you are **confused**, you do not understand what is happening, or you do not know what to do.
વ્યગ્ર, વ્યાકુળ
*She was **confused** about where to go.*

consonant *noun*
consonants

A **consonant** is any letter of the alphabet that is not a, e, i, o, or u.
વ્યંજન
*The word "book" has two **consonants** in it.*

container *noun*
containers

A **container** is something that you use to keep things in, for example a box or a bottle.
પાત્ર

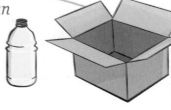

a
b
c
d
e
f
g
h
i
j
k
l
m
n
o
p
q
r
s
t
u
v
w
x
y
z

control *verb*
controls, controlling, controlled

If you **control** something, you can make it do what you want.

અંકુશ હોવો કે રાખવો, કાબુ રાખવો

*I can **control** the speed by pressing this button.*

cook *verb*
cooks, cooking, cooked

When you **cook** food, you make it hot and get it ready to eat.

રાંધવું

*Mum was **cooking** dinner.*

cooker *noun*
cookers

A **cooker** is a machine that you use to cook food.

વરાળથી રાંધવાનું વાસણ, કુકર, રાંધવાને યોગ્ય ફળ

cool *adjective*
cooler, coolest

Something that is **cool** is quite cold.

ઠંડું

*Put the milk in the fridge to keep it **cool**.*

copy *noun*
copies

A **copy** is something that is made to look like another thing.

નકલ, પ્રતિકૃતિ

*I made a **copy** of the drawing.*

corn *noun*

Corn is a long vegetable. It is covered with yellow seeds that you eat.

મકાઈ

corner *noun*
corners

A **corner** is a place where two sides join together.

કોણ, ખૂણો

*He stood at the **corner** of the street.*

correct *adjective*

If something is **correct**, there are no mistakes in it.

સાચું, ખરું

cost *noun*
costs

The **cost** of something is the amount of money you need to buy it.

કિંમત

*The **cost** of the holiday was too high.*

cot *noun*
cots

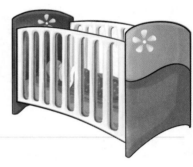

A **cot** is a bed for a baby, with high sides to stop the baby from falling out.

પારણું, ઘોડિયું

cotton *noun*

1 **Cotton** is a kind of cloth that is made from the **cotton** plant.
   કાપડ

2 **Cotton** is also thread that you use to sew with.
   દોરી, ધાગો

cough *verb*
coughs, coughing, coughed

When you **cough**, you make air come out of your throat with a sudden, loud noise.

ઉધરસ ખાવી

*The smoke made us **cough**.*

could *verb*

If you say you **could** do something, you mean that you were able to do it. **Could** comes from the word **can**.

શકવું, સમર્થ હોવું (શબ્દનું ભૂ. કૃ)

*I **could** see through the window.*

couldn't

Couldn't is short for **could not**.

ન કરી શકવું

*She **couldn't** open the door.*

count *verb*
counts, counting, counted

1 When you **count**, you say numbers in order, one after the other.
ગણવું, ગણતરી કરવી
*I **counted** from one to ten.*

2 When you **count** all the things in a group, you add them up to see how many there are.
ગણવામાં,
*The teacher **counted** the children in the class.*

country *noun*
countries

1 A **country** is a part of the world with its own people and laws.
પ્રદેશ, દેશ
*He lives in a different **country**.*

2 The **country** is land that is away from towns and cities. There are farms and woods in the **country**.
ગ્રામીણ પ્રદેશ
*We went for a walk in the **country**.*

cousin *noun*
cousins

Your **cousin** is the son or daughter of your uncle or aunt.
કાકા-મામા કે ફોઈ-માસીનું સંતાન, પિતરાઈ

cover *verb*
covers, covering, covered

If you **cover** something, you put another thing over it.
ઢાંકી દેવું, ઢાંકવું
*She **covered** the table with a cloth.*

cover *noun*
covers

A **cover** is something that you put over another thing.
આચ્છાદન
*Put a **cover** over the sofa to keep it clean.*

cow *noun*
cows

A **cow** is a large animal that is kept on farms because it gives milk.
ગાય

crab *noun*
crabs

A **crab** is an animal with a hard shell that lives in the sea. **Crabs** have large claws on their front legs.
કરચલો

crack *verb*
cracks, cracking, cracked

If something **cracks**, it becomes damaged, and lines appear on the surface where it has broken.
તિરાડ પડવી કે તિરાડ
*The window **cracked**.*

crane *noun*
cranes

1 A **crane** is a tall machine that can lift very heavy things.
ઊંટડો

2 A **crane** is also a large bird with a long neck and long legs. **Cranes** live near water.
બગલું, સારસ

crash *noun*
crashes

1 A **crash** is an accident when a vehicle hits something.
મોટરની સામસામી
*There was a car **crash** outside the school.*

2 A **crash** is also a sudden, loud noise.
ધડાકો
*He dropped the plates with a **crash**.*

crawl *verb*
crawls, crawling, crawled

When you **crawl**, you move along on your hands and knees.
કોણી કે ઢીંચણ પર ઘસડાતા આગળ વધવું
*The baby **crawled** along the floor.*

crayon *noun*
crayons

Crayons are pencils or sticks of wax in different colours that you use for drawing.
ચિત્રકલા માટેનો મીણયુક્ત રંગીન ચોક - ક્રેયોન

cream *noun*

Cream is a thick liquid that is made from milk. You can use it in cooking or pour it over puddings.
મલાઈ

creature noun
creatures

A **creature** is anything that is alive, but is not a plant.
માનવી, કોઈનું આશ્રિત કે હથિયાર, પામર જીવ
*Many **creatures** live in the forest.*

creep verb
creeps, creeping, crept

1 If you **creep** somewhere, you move in a very slow and quiet way.
ધીમેધીમે કે ચોરીચૂપકીથી ખસવું
*He **crept** up the stairs.*

2 If an animal **creeps**, it moves along close to the ground.
પેટે ચાલવું
*The mouse **crept** across the room.*

crew noun
crews

A **crew** is a group of people who work together on a ship or an aeroplane.
જહાજ, હવાઈ જહાજ ઈ.માં કામ કરતા માણસો કે માણસ

cricket noun
crickets

1 **Cricket** is a game where two teams take turns to hit a ball with a bat and run up and down.
ગેડીદડાના જેવી એક રમત, ક્રિકેટ

2 A **cricket** is also a small jumping insect that rubs its wings together to make a high sound.
કંસારી

cried

⇨ Look at **cry**.
*The baby **cried** for its mother.*

cries

⇨ Look at **cry**.
*She always **cries** at sad films.*

crocodile noun
crocodiles

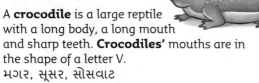

A **crocodile** is a large reptile with a long body, a long mouth and sharp teeth. **Crocodiles'** mouths are in the shape of a letter V.
મગર, સૂસર, સોસવાટ

crop noun
crops

Crops are plants that people grow for food, for example potatoes and wheat.
પાક, પેદાશ

cross verb
crosses, crossing, crossed

If you **cross** something, you go from one side of it to the other.
ઓળંગવું
Cross the road where it is safe.

cross noun
crosses

A **cross** is a mark that you write. It looks like ×.
ચોકડી
*She put a **cross** beside my name.*

cross adjective
crosser, crossest

If you are **cross**, you feel angry about something.
ચીઢિયું, ગુસ્સે થયેલું
*Mum was **cross** because we were late.*

crowd noun
crowds

A **crowd** is a lot of people together in one place.
ટોળું, સમુદાય, ભીડ, ગિરદી
*A big **crowd** came to see the game.*

crown noun
crowns

A **crown** is a circle made of gold or silver and jewels that kings and queens wear on their heads.
તાજ, મુગટ, મુકુટ

cry verb
cries, crying, cried

When you **cry**, tears come from your eyes. People **cry** when they are sad or hurt.
રડવું
*The baby started to **cry**.*

cry *noun*
cries

A **cry** is a loud sound that you make with your voice.
ચીસ,પક્ષીઓનો અવાજ,
*I heard the **cry** of a bird.*

cub *noun*
cubs

A **cub** is a young wild animal, for example a young bear or lion.
સિંહ, વરુ કે રીંછનું બચ્ચું

cube *noun*
cubes

A **cube** is a solid shape with six sides that are all squares.
છ સરખી બાજુઓવાળી ધન આકૃતિ, ધન
*A dice is in the shape of a **cube**.*

cucumber *noun*
cucumbers

A **cucumber** is a long, thin, green vegetable that you eat in salads.
કાકડી

cuddle *verb*
cuddles, cuddling, cuddled

If you **cuddle** someone, you put your arms around them and hold them close to you.
પંપાળવું

cup *noun*
cups

A **cup** is a small, round container with a handle. You drink things like tea and coffee from a **cup**.
પવાલું, પ્યાલો, કપ,

cupboard *noun*
cupboards

A **cupboard** is a piece of furniture with a door and shelves that you keep things in.
કબાટ, અલમારી
*The **cupboard** was full of toys.*

curl *noun*
curls

A **curl** is a piece of hair that has a curved shape.
વાંકડિયા વાળની લટ
*The girl had long, black **curls**.*

curtain *noun*
curtains

A **curtain** is a piece of cloth that you pull across a window to cover it.
પડદો

curved *adjective*

If something is **curved**, it has the shape of a bent line.
વળેલું
*The bird had a **curved** beak.*

cushion *noun*
cushions

A **cushion** is a bag of soft material that you put on a seat to make it more comfortable.
ઉશીકું, તકિયો

customer *noun*
customers

A **customer** is a person who buys something in a shop.
ખરીદનાર, ધરાક, ગ્રાહક

cut *verb*
cuts, cutting, cut

1   If you **cut** something, you use a knife or scissors to divide it into pieces.
    કાપવું
    *We **cut** the cake.*

2   If you **cut** yourself, something sharp goes through your skin and blood comes out.
    ઈજા કરવી
    *Don't **cut** yourself on the broken glass.*

cut *noun*
cuts

A **cut** is a place on your skin where something sharp has gone through it.
કાપવાથી થયેલો જખમ
*He had a **cut** on his cheek.*

a
b
c
d
e
f
g
h
i
j
k
l
m
n
o
p
q
r
s
t
u
v
w
x
y
z

A
B
C
D
E
F
G
H
I
J
K
L
M
N
O
P
Q
R
S
T
U
V
W
X
Y
Z

dad or daddy *noun*
dads or daddies

Dad or **daddy** is a name for your father.
બાપ, પિતા

damage *verb*
damages, damaging, damaged

If you **damage** something, you break it or spoil it.
નુકસાન કરવું
*The storm **damaged** the roof.*

damp *adjective*
damper, dampest

Something that is **damp** is a little bit wet.
સહેજ ભેજ વાળું, હવાયેલું
*Her hair was **damp**.*

dance *verb*
dances, dancing, danced

When you **dance**, you move your body to music.
નાચવું

danger *noun*
dangers

If there is **danger**, something bad might happen to hurt you.
જોખમ
*There is a **danger** that he will fall.*

dangerous *adjective*
If something is **dangerous**, it can hurt you or kill you.
જોખમી
*It is **dangerous** to cross the road here.*

dark *adjective*
darker, darkest

1   When it is **dark**, there is no light or not much light.
અંધારું

2   A **dark** colour is not pale.
ગાઢું, ઘેરું
*She wore a **dark** blue skirt.*

date *noun*
dates

A **date** is the day, the month, and sometimes the year when something happens.
તારીખ
*What **date** is your birthday?*

daughter *noun*
daughters

Someone's **daughter** is their female child.
પુત્રી, દીકરી

day *noun*
days

1   A **day** is the length of time between one midnight and the next. There are twenty-four hours in a **day**, and seven **days** in a week.
મધરાતથી મધરાત
*It is three **days** until my birthday.*

2   **Day** is the time when there is light outside.
દિવસ
*I've been busy all **day**.*

dead *adjective*
A person, an animal, or a plant that is **dead** has stopped living.
મરી ગયેલું, મૃત

deaf *adjective*
Someone who is **deaf** cannot hear anything, or cannot hear very well.
બહેરું

December *noun*
December is the month after November and before January. It has 31 days.
ડિસેમ્બર

decide verb
decides, deciding, decided
When you **decide** to do something, you think about it and then choose to do it.
નક્કી કરવું
*She **decided** to go home.*

decorate verb
decorates, decorating, decorated
If you **decorate** a room, you put paint or paper on its walls.
સુશોભિત કરવું
*We **decorated** the bedroom.*

deep adjective
deeper, deepest
If something is **deep**, it goes down a long way.
ઊંડું
*We dug a **deep** hole in the sand.*

deer noun
deer
A **deer** is a large animal that lives in forests and can run very fast. Male **deer** have big horns that look like branches on their heads.
હરણ

defend verb
defends, defending, defended
If you **defend** someone, you keep them safe from danger.
બચાવવું
*The soldiers **defended** the king.*

delicious adjective
If food is **delicious**, it tastes or smells very good.
સ્વાદિષ્ટ

deliver verb
delivers, delivering, delivered
If you **deliver** something, you take it to someone.
પહોંચાડવું, સુપરત કરવું
*Please **deliver** this letter to him.*

dentist noun
dentists
A **dentist** is a person whose job is to take care of people's teeth.
દાંતનો ડૉક્ટર

depth noun
depths
The **depth** of something is how far down it goes from its top to its bottom.
ઊંડાણ
*The **depth** of the pond is two metres.*

describe verb
describes, describing, described
If you **describe** something, you say what it is like.
વર્ણન કરવું
*He **described** the picture to me.*

desert noun
deserts
A **desert** is a large, dry area of land with almost no trees or plants. **Deserts** are very hot and are often covered with sand.
રણ

desk noun
desks
A **desk** is a kind of table that you sit at to write or to work.
મેજ

destroy verb
destroys, destroying, destroyed
If you **destroy** something, you damage it so much that it cannot be used any more.
નષ્ટ કરવું
*The fire **destroyed** the house.*

a
b
c
d
e
f
g
h
i
j
k
l
m
n
o
p
q
r
s
t
u
v
w
x
y
z

35

A B C D E F G H I J K L M N O P Q R S T U V W X Y Z

diagram *noun*
diagrams

A **diagram** is a drawing that shows something in a way that is very easy to understand.
આકૃતિ

*He drew me a **diagram** of the engine.*

diamond *noun*
diamonds

1 A **diamond** is a kind of jewel that is hard, clear, and shiny.
હીરો

2 A **diamond** is also a shape with four straight sides.
સમબાજુ

diary *noun*
diaries

A **diary** is a book that you use to write down things that happen to you each day.
રોજનીશી, ડાયરી

dice *noun*
dice

A **dice** is a small cube with a different number of spots on each side. You throw **dice** in some games.
ડાઈસ, જૂગટું રમવાના પાસા

dictionary *noun*
dictionaries

A **dictionary** is a book with a list of words in it. The **dictionary** tells you what these words mean, and shows you how to spell them.
શબ્દકોશ

did
➡ Look at **do**.
*I saw what you **did**.*

didn't

Didn't is short for **did not**.
ન કર્યું

*She **didn't** like the film.*

die *verb*
dies, dying, died

When a person, an animal, or a plant **dies**, they stop living.
મરવું, મૃત્યુ પામવું

*Plants **die** if you don't water them.*

different *adjective*

If two things are **different**, they are not like each other.
જુદં

*The crayons were all in **different** colours.*

difficult *adjective*

If something is **difficult**, it is not easy to do or to understand.
મુશ્કેલ, અઘરું, કઠણ

*The homework was too **difficult** for us.*

dig *verb*
digs, digging, dug

If you **dig**, you make a hole in the ground.
ખોદવું, ખોદી કાઢવું, ખોદકામ કરવું

*We **dug** a hole in the garden.*

digital *adjective*

If a machine is **digital**, it shows or sends information by using numbers.
હજારો નાના સંકેતોની નોંધ કરતું

*We have a new **digital** television.*

dinner *noun*
dinners

Dinner is the main meal of the day.
(સાંજનું) ભોજન

dinosaur *noun*
dinosaurs

Dinosaurs were large animals that lived a very long time ago. **Dinosaurs** were like very big lizards.

લુપ્ત થઈ ગયેલ વિશાળકાય (૨ થી ૮૦ ફૂટની લંબાઈવાળાં) પ્રાણી - ડાઈનોસોર

direction *noun*
directions

1   A **direction** is the way that you go to get to a place.
દિશા

*My house is in this **direction**.*

2   **Directions** are words or pictures that show you how to do something, or how to get somewhere.
માર્ગદર્શન

*He gave me **directions** to the station.*

dirt *noun*

Dirt is anything that is not clean, for example, dust or mud.
રજ, ધૂળ, કચરો

*She had **dirt** on her face.*

dirty *adjective*
dirtier, dirtiest

If something is **dirty**, it has mud, food, or other marks on it.
મેલું, બગડેલું, અસ્વચ્છ

*The dishes were **dirty**.*

disappear *verb*
disappears, disappearing, disappeared

If something **disappears**, you cannot see it any more.
અદ્રશ્ય થવું, અલોપ થવું

*The cat **disappeared** under the bed.*

disappointed *adjective*

If you are **disappointed**, you are sad because something you hoped for did not happen.
નિરાશ થયેલ

*I was **disappointed** that you weren't there.*

disaster *noun*
disasters

A **disaster** is something very bad that happens suddenly and that may hurt many people.
હોનારત, અણધારી મહાન આફત

discover *verb*
discovers, discovering, discovered

When you **discover** something, you get to know about it for the first time.
શોધી કાઢવું

*We **discovered** that he was very good at football.*

discuss *verb*
discusses, discussing, discussed

When people **discuss** something, they talk about it together.
ચર્ચા કરવી

*We **discussed** what to do next.*

disease *noun*
diseases

A **disease** is something that makes you ill.
રોગ

*Measles is a **disease**.*

disguise *noun*
disguises

A **disguise** is something you wear so that people will not know who you are.
દેખાવ બદલવો

dish *noun*
dishes

A **dish** is a container that you use to cook or serve food in.
થાળી

disk *noun*
disks

A **disk** is a flat piece of metal and plastic that you use in a computer to store information.
ચપટી સપાટ તકતી

A B C D E F G H I J K L M N O P Q R S T U V W X Y Z

distance *noun*
distances

The **distance** between two things is how much space there is between them.
અંતર
*Measure the **distance** between the wall and the table.*

dive *verb*
dives, diving, dived

If you **dive** into water, you jump in so that your arms and your head go in first.
પાણીમાં ભૂસકો કે ડૂબકી મારવી

divide *verb*
divides, dividing, divided

1 If you **divide** something, you make it into smaller pieces.
ભાગ પાડવા
***Divide** the cake into four pieces.*

2 When you **divide** numbers, you see how many times one number goes into another number.
ભાગાકાર કરવો
*If you **divide** ten by five, you get two.*

do *verb*
does, doing, did, done

If you **do** something, you spend some time on it or finish it.
કરવું
*I tried to **do** some work.*

doctor *noun*
doctors

A **doctor** is a person whose job is to help people who are ill or hurt to get better.
દાકતર, ડૉકટર, તબીબ

does

➡ Look at **do**.
*She **does** her homework before dinner.*

doesn't

Doesn't is short for **does not**.
નથી કરતું
*He **doesn't** like carrots.*

dog *noun*
dogs

A **dog** is an animal that barks. Some **dogs** do special jobs, like helping blind people.
કૂતરો

doing

➡ Look at **do**.
*What are you **doing**?*

doll *noun*
dolls

A **doll** is a toy that looks like a small person or a baby.
ઢીંગલી, પૂતળી

dolphin *noun*
dolphins

A **dolphin** is an animal that lives in the sea and looks like a large fish with a long nose. **Dolphins** are very clever.
એક દરિયાઈ પ્રાણી, ડૉલ્ફિન

done

➡ Look at **do**.
*She has **done** a drawing.*

donkey *noun*
donkeys

A **donkey** is an animal that looks like a small horse with long ears.
ગધેડો

don't

Don't is short for **do not**.
નું દેકુ ૩૫
I **don't** feel well.

door *noun*
doors

You open and close a **door** to get into a building, a room, or a cupboard.
દરવાજો, બારણું

double *adjective*

Double means two times as big, or two times as much.
બમણું, બે ગણું
His room is **double** the size of mine.

down

When something moves **down**, it goes from a higher place to a lower place.
નીચે
She came **down** the stairs.

drag *verb*
drags, dragging, dragged

If you **drag** something, you pull it along the ground.
મુશ્કેલીથી ખેંચવું
He **dragged** his chair to the table.

dragon *noun*
dragons

In stories, a **dragon** is a monster that has wings and can make fire come out of its mouth.
મોંઢેથી આગની ઝાળો કાઢતું સર્પ કે મગર જેવું એક કાલ્પનિક પ્રાણી

drain *verb*
drains, draining, drained

If you **drain** a liquid, you take it away by making it flow to another place.
ખાલી કરવું, નિકાલ કરવો
They **drained** the water out of the tunnel.

drank

⇨ Look at **drink**.
She **drank** a bottle of water.

draw *verb*
draws, drawing, drew, drawn

When you **draw**, you use pens, pencils, or crayons to make a picture.
ચિતરવું
He likes to **draw** animals.

drawer *noun*
drawers

A **drawer** is a box that fits inside a piece of furniture. You can pull it out and put things in it.
ટેબલનું ખાનું

drawing *noun*
drawings

A **drawing** is a picture you make with pens, pencils, or crayons.
દોરેલું ચિત્ર, ચિત્રાલેખન

drawn

⇨ Look at **draw**.
I have **drawn** my house.

dream *noun*
dreams

A **dream** is something you see and hear in your mind while you are sleeping.
સ્વપ્ન
I had a **dream** about winning the prize.

dress *noun*
dresses

A **dress** is something a girl or a woman can wear. It covers the body and part of the legs.
ફરાક
She wore a yellow **dress**.

dress *verb*
dresses, dressing, dressed

When you **dress**, you put on clothes.
કપડાં પહેરવાં
He **dressed** quickly because he was late.

drew
⇨ Look at **draw**.
She **drew** a picture of a horse.

drink *verb*
drinks, drinking, drank, drunk

When you **drink**, you swallow liquid.
પીવું
Mum **drinks** a lot of coffee.

drip *verb*
drips, dripping, dripped

When liquid **drips**, a small amount of it falls from somewhere.
ટીપાં પડવાં
Water **dripped** from the roof.

drive *verb*
drives, driving, drove, driven

When someone **drives** a vehicle, they make it go where they want.
(ગાડી, મોટર,ઇ.) હંકવું, ચલાવવું
He knows how to **drive** a car.

drop *verb*
drops, dropping, dropped

If you **drop** something, you let it fall.
હાથમાંથી છોડી દેવું
I **dropped** a plate on the floor.

drove
⇨ Look at **drive**.
We **drove** to the shops.

drown *verb*
drowns, drowning, drowned

If someone **drowns**, they die because their face is below water and they cannot breathe.
ડૂબવું, ડૂબીને મરી જવું

drum *noun*
drums

A **drum** is an instrument that you hit with sticks or with your hands to make music.
ઢોલ, નગારું, પડઘમ

drunk
⇨ Look at **drink**.
Have you **drunk** all the milk?

dry *adjective*
drier, driest

If something is **dry**, there is no water in it or on it.
કોરું
My clothes are **dry**.

duck *noun*
ducks

A **duck** is a bird that lives near water and can swim. **Ducks** have large flat beaks.
બતક

dug
⇨ Look at **dig**.
We **dug** a hole in the sand.

dull *adjective*
duller, dullest

1 Something that is **dull** is not interesting.
કંટાળાજનક
That was a very **dull** book.

2 A **dull** colour is not bright.
ઝાંખું
He wore a **dull** green jacket.

dust *noun*

Dust is tiny pieces of dry dirt that looks like powder.
ધૂળ, રજ
The table was covered in **dust**.

each

Each means every one.
દરેક જણ, પ્રત્યેક
*He gave **each** of us a book.*

eagle *noun*
eagles

An **eagle** is a large bird with a curved beak and sharp claws. **Eagles** eat small animals.
ગરુડ

ear *noun*
ears

Your **ears** are the two parts of your body that you hear sounds with.
કાન
*He whispered something in her **ear**.*

early *adjective*
earlier, earliest

1 If you are **early**, you arrive before the time that you were expected to come.
નિયત સમય પહેલાં
*She was too **early** for the party.*

2 **Early** also means near the first part of something.
જલદી
*I got up **early** in the morning.*

earn *verb*
earns, earning, earned

If you **earn** money, you work to get it.
કમાણી થવી
*He **earned** some money washing the car.*

earth *noun*

1 The **Earth** is the planet that we live on.
પૃથ્વી

2 **Earth** is also the soil that plants grow in.
જમીન, ધરતી

earthquake *noun*
earthquakes

When there is an **earthquake**, the ground shakes and buildings often fall down.
ધરતીકંપ

east *noun*

The **east** is the direction that is in front of you when you are looking towards the place where the sun rises.
પૂર્વ દિશા

easy *adjective*
easier, easiest

If something is **easy**, you can do it or understand it without having to try very much.
સહેલું
*These sums are **easy**.*

eat *verb*
eats, eating, ate, eaten

When you **eat**, you chew and swallow food.
ખાવું
*She **eats** too many sweets.*

echo *noun*
echoes

An **echo** is a sound that you hear again because it bounces off something solid and then comes back.
પડઘો
*We heard the **echo** of our voices in the cave.*

A
B
C
D
E
F
G
H
I
J
K
L
M
N
O
P
Q
R
S
T
U
V
W
X
Y
Z

edge *noun*
edges

The **edge** of something is the part along the end or side of it.
ને છેવાડે
*She stood at the **edge** of the pond.*

effect *noun*
effects

An **effect** is something that happens because of another thing.
અસર
*The flood was an **effect** of all the rain.*

effort *noun*
efforts

If you make an **effort** to do something, you have to work a lot to do it.
પ્રયત્ન
*She made an **effort** to win the race.*

egg *noun*
eggs

Baby birds, insects, and some other animals live in **eggs** until they are big enough to come out and be born. People often eat hens' **eggs** as food.
ઇંડું

eight *noun*

Eight is the number .
આઠ

elbow *noun*
elbows

Your **elbow** is the part in the middle of your arm where it bends.
કોણી
*She put her **elbows** on the table.*

electricity *noun*

Electricity is a kind of energy that is used to make light, to make things hot, and to make machines work.
વીજળી

elephant *noun*
elephants

An **elephant** is a very large, grey animal with big ears, a long nose called a trunk, and two long, curved teeth called tusks.
હાથી

eleven *noun*

Eleven is the number **11**.
અગિયાર

email or e-mail *noun*

An **email** is a message like a letter that you send from one computer to another.
કમ્પ્યૂટર દ્વારા સંદેશ
*I got an **email** from my cousin.*

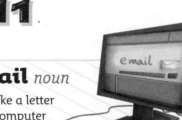

empty *adjective*
emptier, emptiest

If something is **empty**, there is nothing inside it.
ખાલી
*The bottle was **empty**.*

encyclopedia *noun*
encyclopedias

An **encyclopedia** is a book that gives you information about many different things.
જ્ઞાનકોશ

end *noun*
ends

The **end** of something is the last part of it.
અંત, છેડો
*He told me the **end** of the story.*

enemy *noun*
enemies

If someone is your **enemy**, they hate you and want to hurt you.
દુશ્મન

42

energy *noun*

1 If you have **energy**, you have the strength to move around a lot and do things.
તાકાત
*He has the **energy** to run for miles.*

2 **Energy** is also the power that makes machines work.
શક્તિ, ઊર્જા
*The lamp gets its **energy** from the sun.*

engine *noun*
engines

1 An **engine** is a machine that makes things like cars and planes move.
યંત્ર

2 An **engine** is also the front part of a train that pulls it along.
એંજિન

enjoy *verb*
enjoys, enjoying, enjoyed

If you **enjoy** something, you like doing it.
આનંદ કરવો
*I **enjoy** reading.*

enormous *adjective*

Something that is **enormous** is very big.
પ્રચંડ
*Whales are **enormous**.*

enough

If you have **enough** of something, you have as much as you need.
પૂરતું
*I don't have **enough** money to buy both books.*

enter *verb*
enters, entering, entered

When you **enter** a place, you go into it.
પ્રવેશવું

entrance *noun*
entrances

The **entrance** of a place is the way you get into it.
પ્રવેશ દ્વાર
*We found the **entrance** to the tunnel.*

envelope *noun*
envelopes

An **envelope** is a paper cover that you put a letter or a card into before you send it to someone.
કવર

environment *noun*

The **environment** is the land, water, and air around us.
વાતાવરણ
*We must try to protect the **environment**.*

equal *adjective*

If two things are **equal**, they are the same in size, number, or amount.
સમાન, સરખું
*Mix **equal** amounts of milk and water.*

equipment *noun*

Equipment is all the things that you need to do something.
સાધનસામગ્રી
*He put his football **equipment** in his bag.*

escape *verb*
escapes, escaping, escaped

If a person or an animal **escapes**, they get away from somewhere.
નાશી જવું
*My guinea pig **escaped** from its cage.*

even *adjective*

1 An **even** number is a number that you can divide by two, with nothing left over.
સરખું, સમાન
*Four is an **even** number.*

2 Something that is **even** is flat and smooth.
સપાટ
*The path was straight and **even**.*

a
b
c
d
e
f
g
h
i
j
k
l
m
n
o
p
q
r
s
t
u
v
w
x
y
z

A
B
C
D
E
F
G
H
I
J
K
L
M
N
O
P
Q
R
S
T
U
V
W
X
Y
Z

evening *noun*
evenings

The **evening** is the part of each day between the end of the afternoon and the time when people usually go to bed.
સાંજ

ever

Ever means at any time.
ક્યારેય

*Have you **ever** seen anything like it?*

every *adjective*

You use **every** to mean all the people or things in a group.
દરેક

Every pupil in the school was there.

everybody

Everybody means all the people in a group, or all the people in the world.
દરેક જણ

Everybody likes him.

everyone

Everyone means all the people in a group, or all the people in the world.
બધા, એકેએક જણ

Everyone knows who she is.

everything

Everything means all of something.
તમામ બાબત

*He told me **everything** that happened.*

everywhere

Everywhere means in every place.
બધે ઠેકાણે, સર્વત્ર

*I looked **everywhere** for my keys.*

example *noun*
examples

An **example** is something that you use to show what other things in the same group are like.
ઉદાહરણ

*Here is an **example** of my drawings.*

excellent *adjective*

Something that is **excellent** is very good.
બહુ જ સારું

*It was an **excellent** film.*

excited *adjective*

If you are **excited**, you are very happy about something and you keep thinking about it.
ઉત્સુક

*He was very **excited** about going to the beach.*

excuse *noun*
excuses

An **excuse** is a reason that you give to explain why you did something.
બહાનું

*She had a good **excuse** for being late.*

exercise *noun*
exercises

1 When you do **exercise**, you move your body so that you can keep healthy and strong.
કસરત, વ્યાયામ
*Running and swimming are both good **exercise**.*

2 An **exercise** is also something you do to practise what you have learnt.
મહાવરો, અભ્યાસ
*We did a maths **exercise**.*

exit *noun*
exits

The **exit** of a building is the door you use to get out of it.
એક્ઝિટ -બહાર જવાનો રસ્તો
*We left by the nearest **exit**.*

expect verb
expects, expecting, expected

If you **expect** something to happen, you think that it will happen.
ધારવું, આશારાખવી
I expect that he will come.

expensive adjective

If something is **expensive**, you need a lot of money to buy it.
મોંઘું

explain verb
explains, explaining, explained

If you **explain** something, you talk about it so that people can understand it.
સમજાવવું
He explained to me how the machine worked.

explode verb
explodes, exploding, exploded

If something **explodes**, it bursts with a very loud noise.
વિસ્ફોટ થવો

explore verb
explores, exploring, explored

If you **explore** a place, you look around it to see what it is like.
ધૂમવું-ખૂંદવું
We explored the old castle.

extinct adjective

If an animal or a plant is **extinct**, there are none of them alive any more.
લુપ્ત
Dinosaurs are extinct.

extra adjective

Extra means more than the usual amount.
વધારાનું
I wore an extra jumper because it was cold.

eye noun
eyes

Your **eyes** are the parts of your body that you see with.
આંખ
I opened my eyes and looked.

Ff

face noun
faces

Your **face** is the front part of your head.
મોઢું, ચહેરો
She has a beautiful face.

fact noun
facts

A **fact** is something that you know is true.
હકીકત, વાસ્તવિકતા

factory noun
factories

A **factory** is a large building where people use machines to make things.
કારખાનું
He works in a factory that makes computers.

fail verb
fails, failing, failed

If you **fail**, you try to do something but you cannot do it.
ભાંગી પડવું, નિષ્ફળ જવું, નાપાસ થવું
She failed to find her lost keys.

fair adjective
fairer, fairest

1 If something is **fair**, it seems right because it is the same for everyone.
વ્યાજબી, ન્યાયી
It's not fair – he's got more than me!

2 **Fair** hair is pale yellow in colour.
આછું ગોરું

fairy *noun*
fairies

In stories, **fairies** are tiny creatures with wings who can do magic.
જાદુઈ શક્તિ ધરાવતી,નાજુક, કાલ્પનિક સ્ત્રી

fall *verb*
falls, falling, fell, fallen

If a person or thing **falls**, they move towards the ground suddenly by accident.
નીચે પડવું
*He **fell** off his bike.*

fallen

⇨ Look at **fall**.
*An apple had **fallen** from the tree.*

family *noun*
families

A **family** is a group of people made up of parents and their children. Aunts and uncles, cousins, grandmothers, and grandfathers are also part of your **family**.
કુટુંબ

famous *adjective*

If someone is **famous**, a lot of people know who they are.
સારી પેઠે જાણીતું, પ્રખ્યાત, સરસ
*She wants to be rich and **famous**.*

far
farther, farthest

If something is **far** away, it is a long way away.
દૂર, આઘે
*His house was **far** away.*

farm *noun*
farms

A **farm** is a piece of land with buildings on it where people grow crops and keep animals.
ખેતર, પાક લેવા કે પ્રાણીઓ ઉછેરવાં માટેની જમીન

farmer *noun*
farmers

A **farmer** is a person who grows crops and keeps animals on a farm.
ખેડૂત

fast *adjective*
faster, fastest

Something that is **fast** can move quickly.
ઝડપથી
*This car is very **fast**.*

fasten *verb*
fastens, fastening, fastened

When you **fasten** something, you close it up.
બંધ કરવું
*She **fastened** the buttons on her coat.*

fat *adjective*
fatter, fattest

Someone who is **fat** has a big, round body.
જાડું

father *noun*
fathers

A **father** is a man who has a child.
પિતા, વડવો

fault *noun*
faults

If something bad is your **fault**, you made it happen.
દોષ, ખોડ, ખામી,
*It's my **fault** that we were late.*

favourite *adjective*

Your **favourite** person or thing is the one you like best.
માનીતું,વધુ વહાલું કે પસંદ
*My **favourite** food is cheese.*

fear *noun*

Fear is the way you feel when you think that something bad is going to happen to you.
ડર, ભય,બીક
*She shook with **fear**.*

feast *noun*
feasts

A **feast** is a large and special meal for a lot of people.
ઉજાણી

feather *noun*
feathers

Feathers are the soft, light things that cover a bird's body. They keep the bird warm and help it to fly.
પીંછું, પર, પીંછાં

February *noun*

February is the month after January and before March. It usually has 28 days, but once every four years, it has 29 days.
ફેબ્રુઅરી, વર્ષનો બીજો મહિનો

feed *verb*
feeds, feeding, fed

If you **feed** a person or an animal, you give them food.
ખાવાનું આપવું, ખવડાવવું
*I **feed** my cat twice a day.*

feel *verb*
feels, feeling, felt

1 The way you **feel**, for example happy or sad, or cold or tired, is how you are at the time.
લાગવું
*I **feel** very upset.*

2 If you **feel** something, you touch it with your hand to see what it is like.
સ્પર્શ કરીને જાણવું
***Feel** how soft these feathers are.*

feet
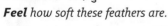 Look at **foot**.
*Don't put your **feet** on the chair.*

fell
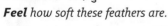 Look at **fall**.
*She **fell** and hurt her knee.*

felt
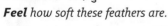 Look at **feel**.
*I **felt** angry.*

female *adjective*

A **female** person or animal could become a mother.
નારી જાતિનું, સ્ત્રી જાતિનું

fence *noun*
fences

A **fence** is a wall made of wood or metal that goes round a piece of land.
ખેતર ફરતી તારની વાડ
*There is a **fence** round the garden.*

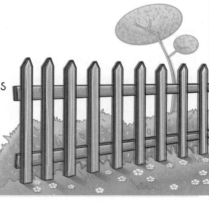

fetch *verb*
fetches, fetching, fetched

If you **fetch** something, you go to where it is and bring it back.
જઈને લાવવું, લઈ આવવું,
*He **fetched** a towel from the bathroom.*

fever *noun*
fevers

If you have a **fever** when you are ill, your body is too hot.
તાવ, જ્વર, તાવ આણવો

few
fewer, fewest

A **few** means some, but not many.
બહુ જ થોડું, જૂજ
*She gave me a **few** sweets.*

A B C D E F G H I J K L M N O P Q R S T U V W X Y Z

field noun
fields

A **field** is a piece of land where people grow crops or keep animals.
જમીન (નો ટુકડો), ધરતી ખાસ કરીને ગોચરની કે ખેડાણ

fierce adjective
fiercer, fiercest

A **fierce** animal is very angry and might attack you.
હિંસક, ઉગ્ર, તીવ્ર, વિકરાળ
*That dog looks very **fierce**.*

fight verb
fights, fighting, fought

When people **fight**, they try to hurt each other.
ઝઘડો, ઝપાઝપી,
*Two boys started to **fight** in the playground.*

fill verb
fills, filling, filled

If you **fill** something, you put so much into it that you cannot get any more in.
ભરવું, ભરાઈ જવું, પૂર્તિ કરવી
*She **filled** her cup with tea.*

film noun
films

A **film** is a story told in moving pictures that you watch on a screen.
ચિત્રપટ, ફિલ્મ પર ઉતારેલી વાર્તા

fin noun
fins

A **fin** is one of the thin, flat parts on a fish's body that help it to swim.
માછલી ઇ.નો પાંખ કે હાથ જેવો અવયવ

find verb
finds, finding, found

If you **find** something that has been lost, you see it after you have been looking for it.
ખોળવું, શોધવું, ખોળી કાઢવું
*I can't **find** my shoes.*

fine adjective
finer, finest

1   If you say that you are **fine**, you mean that you are well or happy.
સરસ, ઉમદા
*I feel **fine** now.*

2   Something that is **fine** is very thin.
સૂક્ષ્મ, બારીક
*She sewed the cloth with **fine** thread.*

3   When the weather is **fine**, it is dry and sunny.
વરસાદ રહીત ચોખ્ખી નિર્મળ હવા
*It is a **fine** day.*

finger noun
fingers

Your **fingers** are the long thin parts at the end of each hand.
આંગળી
*She put the ring on her **finger**.*

finish verb
finishes, finishing, finished

When you **finish** something, you come to the end of it.
પૂરું કરવું
*I **finished** my homework.*

fire noun
fires

Fire is the hot, bright flames that come from something that is burning.
અગ્નિ, જ્વાળા
*The **fire** destroyed the forest.*

fire engine noun
fire engines

A **fire engine** is a large truck that carries people and equipment to stop fires.
આગ હોલવવાનો બંબો

firework noun
fireworks

Fireworks are things that make a loud bang or flashes of bright colour when they are burned.
દારૂખાનું

firm *adjective*
firmer, firmest
Something that is **firm** is hard, and is not easy to bend.
કઠણ

first *adjective*
If a person or thing is **first**, they come before all the others.
પહેલું, પ્રથમ
*January is the **first** month of the year.*

fish *noun*
fish, fishes

A **fish** is an animal that lives in water. **Fish** have fins to help them swim.
માછલી

fit *verb*
fits, fitting, fitted
If something **fits** you, it is the right size and shape for you.
યોગ્ય, લાયક
*These shoes don't **fit** me.*

five *noun*

Five is the number 5.
પાંચ

fix *verb*
fixes, fixing, fixed
1 If you **fix** something that is broken, you mend it.
દુરસ્ત કરવું
*He **fixed** the radio.*

2 If you **fix** something to another thing, you join them together.
જડવું, બેસાડવું
*She **fixed** the shelf to the wall.*

flag *noun*
flags

A **flag** is a piece of cloth with a pattern on it. Each country of the world has its own **flag**.
નિશાન, ઝંડો

flame *noun*
flames
A **flame** is the hot, bright light that comes from a fire.
અગ્નિની જ્વાળા, જ્યોત
*The **flames** almost burned her fingers.*

flash *noun*
flashes

A **flash** is a sudden bright light.
ઝબકારો
*There was a **flash** of lightning.*

flat *adjective*
flatter, flattest
If something is **flat**, it is smooth and does not have any lumps.
સપાટ
*Lay the painting on a **flat** surface until it is dry.*

flavour *noun*
flavours
The **flavour** of food is the taste that it has.
લહેજત, સ્વાદ
*They had ice cream in lots of **flavours**.*

flew
⇨ Look at **fly**.
*An aeroplane **flew** across the sky.*

flies
⇨ Look at **fly**.
*A bird **flies** by moving its wings.*

float *verb*
floats, floating, floated
1 If something **floats** in a liquid, it stays on top of it.
તરવું
*The boat **floated** on the water.*

2 If something **floats** in the air, it moves slowly through it.
(હવામાં) તરવું
*A balloon **floated** over our heads.*

a
b
c
d
e
f
g
h
i
j
k
l
m
n
o
p
q
r
s
t
u
v
w
x
y
z

A B C D E F G H I J K L M N O P Q R S T U V W X Y Z

flock *noun*
flocks

A **flock** is the name for a group of birds or sheep.
એકસાથે રહેતાં ઊડતાં પંખી કે એક સાથે રાખવામાં આવતા પાલતુ જાનવરોનું ટોળું

flood *noun*
floods

If there is a **flood**, a lot of water covers land that is usually dry.
પૂર, રેલ, જલપ્રલય
*We couldn't get to school because of the **flood**.*

floor *noun*
floors

1 A **floor** is the part of a room that you walk on.
ઘર કે ઓરડાની ભોંય
*There were carpets on the **floor**.*

2 A **floor** of a building is all the rooms in it that are at the same height.
માળ, મજલો
*Our house is on the first **floor**.*

flour *noun*

Flour is a powder made from wheat that is used to make bread and cakes.
લોટ

flow *verb*
flows, flowing, flowed

If something **flows**, it moves along in a steady way and does not stop.
વહેવું, (લોહી ઇ. અંગે) બધે ફરવું કે ફરતું રહેવું
*The river **flowed** through the forest.*

flower *noun*
flowers

A **flower** is the part of a plant that makes seeds. **Flowers** often have bright colours and a nice smell.
ફૂલ

flown

⟹ Look at **fly**.
*The birds have all **flown** away.*

flu *noun*

If you have **flu**, you feel as if you have a very bad cold, and your body aches.
એક જાતનો તાવ

fly *verb*
flies, flying, flew, flown

When a bird or aeroplane **flies**, it moves through the air.
ઊડવું

fly *noun*
flies

A **fly** is a small insect with two thin, clear wings.
માખી

fog *noun*

Fog is a thick cloud that is close to the ground. It is hard to see through it.
ધુમ્મસ, ગાઢું ઝાંકળ

fold *verb*
folds, folding, folded

If you **fold** something, you bend it so that one part of it goes over another.
વાળવું, ઘડી કરવી
*He **folded** the letter and put it in the envelope.*

follow *verb*
follows, following, followed

If you **follow** someone, you go along behind them.
અનુસરવું
*We **followed** him up the stairs.*

food *noun*
foods
Food is what people and animals eat.
ખોરાક

foot *noun*
feet
Your **feet** are the parts of your body that are at the ends of your legs, and that you stand on.
પગ, ચરણ
*Stand with one **foot** in front of the other.*

football *noun*
footballs
1 **Football** is a game played by two teams of eleven people who kick a ball and try to score goals by getting the ball into a net.
ફૂટબૉલની રમત

2 A **football** is the ball that you use to play football.
ફૂટબૉલ

forehead *noun*
foreheads
Your **forehead** is the part of your face that is between your hair and your eyes.
કપાળ, લલાટ
*She had a bruise on her **forehead**.*

forest *noun*
forests
A **forest** is a place where a lot of trees grow close together.
વન, જંગલ

forever
If something goes on **forever**, it never comes to an end.
હંમેશાં
*The film seemed to go on **forever**.*

forgave
⇨ Look at **forgive**.
*She **forgave** her brother for spoiling her drawing.*

forget *verb*
forgets, forgetting, forgot, forgotten
If you **forget** something, you do not remember it.
ભૂલી જવું
*Don't **forget** to lock the door.*

forgive *verb*
forgives, forgiving, forgave, forgiven
If you **forgive** someone who has done something bad, you stop being angry with them.
જતું કરવું, માફ કરવું
*Please **forgive** me for being late.*

forgot
⇨ Look at **forget**.
*She **forgot** to bring any money.*

forgotten
⇨ Look at **forget**.
*I have **forgotten** my keys.*

fork *noun*
forks
A **fork** is a tool with three or four thin, sharp points that you use to eat food with.
ખાવા માટે વપરાતો કાંટો

fortnight *noun*
fortnights
A **fortnight** is two weeks.
પખવાડિયું

forwards
If you move **forwards**, you move towards the front.
આગળ
*They ran backwards and **forwards** trying to catch the ball.*

a b c d e f g h i j k l m n o p q r s t u v w x y z

51

fought
⇨ Look at **fight**.
*The knights **fought** with swords.*

found
⇨ Look at **find**.
*She **found** her lost dog.*

four *noun*
Four is the number 4.
ચાર

fox *noun*
foxes
A **fox** is an animal that looks like a dog with red fur and a long, thick tail.
શિયાળ, કોલું

fraction *noun*
fractions
A **fraction** is a part of a whole number.
ખંડ, ટુકડો, અપૂર્ણાંક
*A half and a quarter are both **fractions**.*

frame *noun*
frames
A **frame** is a piece of wood, metal or plastic that fits around the edge of a picture, a window, or a door.
ફ્રેમ, (છબી કે અરિસાની આસપાસનું) ચોકઠું કે ખોખું

frame

freckles *noun*
Freckles are light brown spots that some people have on their skin.
ચામડી પર આછા ભૂરા રંગનું ટપકું કે ડાઘો
*His face was covered with **freckles**.*

free *adjective*
freer, freest
1 If something is **free**, you can have it without paying any money for it.
મફત
*If you buy a cup of coffee, you get a **free** cake.*

2 If you are **free**, you can do what you like or go where you like.
મૂક્ત, સ્વતંત્ર
*You are **free** to come here any time.*

freeze *verb*
freezes, freezing, froze, frozen
1 When water **freezes**, it is so cold that it becomes ice.
જામવું

2 If you **freeze** food, you make it very cold so that it will not go bad.
ઠારવું

fresh *adjective*
fresher, freshest
1 If food is **fresh**, it has been picked or made a short time ago.
તાજું
*Eat some **fresh** fruit every day.*

2 **Fresh** water has no salt in it. The water in rivers is **fresh**.
મીઠું

3 **Fresh** air is clean and cool.
ચોખ્ખી

Friday *noun*
Fridays
Friday is the day after Thursday and before Saturday.
શુક્રવાર
*He went home on **Friday**.*

fridge *noun*
fridges
A **fridge** is a cupboard that uses electricity to keep food cold and fresh.
શીતકબાટ, રેફ્રિજરેટર
*Put the butter in the **fridge**.*

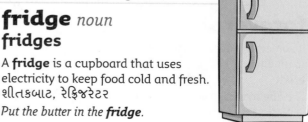

fried
⇨ Look at **fry**.
*She **fried** some eggs.*

friend *noun*
friends
A **friend** is someone you know and like, and who likes you too.
મિત્ર, ભાઈબંધ

friendly *adjective*
friendlier, friendliest
If someone is **friendly**, they like to meet other people, and are nice to them.
મિત્રતાવાળું

frighten *verb*
frightens, frightening, frightened
If something **frightens** you, it makes you feel afraid.
બિવડાવવું, ડરાવવું
*Loud noises **frighten** her.*

frog *noun*
frogs
A **frog** is a small animal with smooth skin, big eyes, and long back legs that it uses for jumping. **Frogs** live near water.
દેડકો

front *noun*
fronts
The **front** of something is the part that comes first or the part that you usually see first.
આગળ
*She stood at the **front** of the queue.*

frost *noun*
Frost is ice that looks like white powder. It covers things outside when the weather is very cold.
હિમ

frown *verb*
frowns, frowning, frowned
When you **frown**, lines appear on your forehead because you are cross or because you are thinking about something.
ભવાં ચડાવવાં, ડોળા કાઢવા, નાખુશી બતાવવી

froze
⇨ Look at **freeze**.
*It was so cold that the lake **froze**.*

frozen
⇨ Look at **freeze**.
*The water had **frozen** into ice.*

fruit *noun*
fruits
Fruit is the part of a plant or a tree that has the seeds in it. You can eat many **fruits**, for example apples, bananas, and strawberries.
ફળ

fry *verb*
fries, frying, fried
When you **fry** food, you cook it in hot oil or butter.
તળવું
Fry the onions until they are brown.

full *adjective*
fuller, fullest
If something is **full**, it has so much in it that it cannot hold any more.
પૂર્ણ, -થી ભરેલું
*The bottle is **full**.*

a
b
c
d
e
f
g
h
i
j
k
l
m
n
o
p
q
r
s
t
u
v
w
x
y
z

fun *noun*

When you have **fun**, you enjoy doing something
and you feel happy.
મોજ, આનંદ

*They had **fun** at the beach.*

funny *adjective*
funnier, funniest

1 If something is **funny**, it makes you laugh.
રમૂજી

   *He told me a **funny** joke.*

2 **Funny** also means strange.
   વિચિત્ર

   *The car is making a **funny** noise.*

fur *noun*

Fur is the soft hair that
covers the bodies of
many animals.
અમુક પ્રાણીઓના સુંવાળા વાળ

*Pandas have black
and white **fur**.*

furniture *noun*

Furniture is the name for all the big things,
for example tables, chairs, or beds,
that people have in their houses.
ઘરનું રાચરચીલું

*We bought new **furniture**
for the bedroom.*

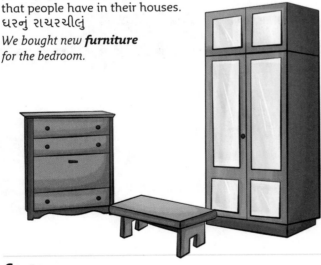

future *noun*

The **future** is the time that will come after the
present time.
હવે પછી બનવાનું કે થવાનું,હોવાનું

*In the **future**, people will travel to other planets.*

gale *noun*
gales

A **gale** is a very strong wind.
સખત પવન, આંધી

game *noun*
games

1 A **game** is something you play that has rules, for
   example football.
   રમત

2 Children also play a **game** when they pretend to
   be other people.
   ગમ્મત

   *We played a **game** of pirates.*

gap *noun*
gaps

A **gap** is a space between two things.
અંતર

*There was a **gap** between the curtains.*

garage *noun*
garages

1 A **garage** is a building
   where you keep a car.
   ગરાજ, મોટર ગાડીઓ
   રાખવાનું સ્થાન/છાપરું

2 A **garage** is also a
   place where you can
   get your car repaired.
   મોટર સમી કરવાની દુકાન

garden *noun*
gardens

A **garden** is a piece of
land near a house where
people can grow grass,
flowers, and vegetables.
બગીચો

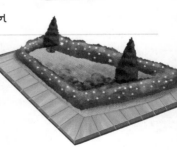

gas *noun*
gases

A **gas** is anything, for example air, that is not solid or a liquid.
વાયુ

gate *noun*
gates

A **gate** is a kind of door in a wall, a fence, or a hedge.
દરવાજો

gave

⇨ Look at **give**.
*She **gave** me a present.*

gentle *adjective*
gentler, gentlest

If you are **gentle**, you are careful and not rough.
કોમળ, મૃદુ, સૌમ્ય
*Be **gentle** when you hold the baby.*

get *verb*
gets, getting, got

1 You can use **get** to mean the same as "become".
થવું
*We should go before it **gets** dark.*

2 If you **get** somewhere, you arrive there.
આવવું
*He **got** home at noon.*

3 If you **get** something, someone gives it to you.
મળવું, મેળવવું
*I **got** a bike for my birthday.*

4 If you **get** something, you go to where it is and bring it back.
લાવવું
*He went to **get** a cup of coffee.*

ghost *noun*
ghosts

A **ghost** is a dead person who some people think they can see and hear.
ભૂત

giant *adjective*

Something that is **giant** is very large.
વિશાળ, વિરાટ
*They watched the film on a **giant** TV screen.*

giraffe *noun*
giraffes

A **giraffe** is a very tall animal with a long neck, long legs, and dark spots on its body.
જિરાફ

girl *noun*
girls

A **girl** is a child or a young person who is a female.
છોકરી

give *verb*
gives, giving, gave, given

If you **give** someone something, you let them have it to keep.
આપવું
*We always **give** our mother flowers on her birthday.*

glad *adjective*
gladder, gladdest

If you are **glad**, you are happy about something.
પ્રસન્ન, ખુશ
*I'm **glad** you can come to my party.*

glass *noun*
glasses

1 **Glass** is a hard, clear material that is used to make things like windows and bottles. It is quite easy to break **glass**.
કાચ
*The salad was in a **glass** bowl.*

2 A **glass** is also a container made from glass that you can drink out of.
પવાલું, પ્યાલો
*He filled his **glass** with milk.*

glasses *noun*

Glasses are two pieces of plastic or glass in a frame that people wear in front of their eyes to help them to see better.
ચશ્મા

a
b
c
d
e
f
g
h
i
j
k
l
m
n
o
p
q
r
s
t
u
v
w
x
y
z

A
B
C
D
E
F
G
H
I
J
K
L
M
N
O
P
Q
R
S
T
U
V
W
X
Y
Z

glove *noun*
gloves

Gloves are things that you wear over your hands to keep them warm. **Gloves** have one part for your thumb and one for all your fingers.
હાથમોજું

glue *noun*

You use **glue** to stick things together.
ગુંદર

go *verb*
goes, going, went, gone

1   If you **go** somewhere, you move there from another place.
જવું
Can we go to the park?

2   If you say that something is **going** to happen, you mean that it will happen.
થવું, બનવું
He's going to leave soon.

goal *noun*
goals

In games like football, the **goal** is the place that you try to get the ball in to, to score a point.
લક્ષ્ય

goat *noun*
goats

A **goat** is an animal about the size of a sheep. **Goats** have horns, and hair on their chin that looks like a beard.
બકરી

gold *noun*

Gold is a valuable, yellow metal that is used to make things like rings and necklaces, and also coins.
સોનું, સુવર્ણ

goldfish *noun*
goldfish

A **goldfish** is a small orange fish that people often keep as a pet.
જર્દ માછલી

gone

⇨ Look at **go**.
She has gone home.

good *adjective*
better, best

1   If you say that something is **good**, you like it.
સારું
That was a good film.

2   If you are **good**, you behave well.
સદ્‍ગુણી, યોગ્ય
Be good while I am out.

3   If you are **good** at something, you do it well.
સરસ, ઉમદા
She is good at drawing.

goodbye

You say **goodbye** to someone when one of you is going away.
આવજો!

good night

You say **good night** to someone late in the evening before you go home or go to bed.
શુભરાત્રિ

goose *noun*
geese

A **goose** is a large bird with a long neck that lives near water.
કલહંસ

gorilla *noun*
gorillas

A **gorilla** is a large, strong animal with long arms, black fur, and a black face.
ગોરિલો

got

⇨ Look at **get**.
They soon got tired of the game.

grain *noun*
grains

1 A **grain** is the seed of a cereal plant, for example rice or wheat.
દાણો

2 A **grain** of something, for example sand or salt, is a tiny piece of it.
દાણો

gram *noun*
grams

A **gram** is used for measuring how heavy things are.
વજનનું માપ

*There are about 400 **grams** of jam in this jar.*

grandfather *noun*
grandfathers

Your **grandfather** is your father's father or your mother's father.
દાદા કે નાના

grandmother *noun*
grandmothers

Your **grandmother** is your father's mother or your mother's mother.
દાદી કે નાની

grape *noun*
grapes

A **grape** is a small, round, green or purple fruit that grows in bunches.
દ્રાક્ષ, અંગૂર

grapefruit *noun*
grapefruits

A **grapefruit** is a large, round, yellow fruit with a sour taste.
મોટા સંતરા જેવું પરંતુ સ્વાદે સહેજ કડછું

graph *noun*
graphs

In maths, a **graph** is a picture that uses lines or shapes to show numbers.
આલેખ

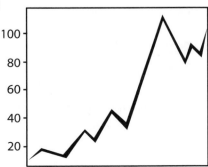

grass *noun*
grasses

Grass is a green plant with very thin leaves that cover the ground in fields and gardens.
ધાસ

great *adjective*
greater, greatest

1 **Great** means very large.
વિશાળ
*The king lived in a **great** palace.*

2 **Great** also means very important.
મહત્ત્વનું
*The computer was a **great** invention.*

3 If you say that something is **great**, you mean that it is very good.
ધણું સારું
*We had a **great** time.*

greedy *adjective*
greedier, greediest

If someone is **greedy**, they want to have more of something than they need.
લાલચી

*He was so **greedy** that he ate the whole cake.*

green *noun*

Green is the colour of grass or leaves.
લીલો રંગ

*Her dress is **green**.*

grew

▷ Look at **grow**.
*The tree **grew** to a great height.*

grey *noun*

Grey is a mixture of black and white, like the colour of clouds when rain is falling.
ભૂખરું

ground *noun*

The **ground** is the earth or other surface that you walk on outside.
જમીન, ધરતી

a b c d e f **g** h i j k l m n o p q r s t u v w x y z

A B C D E F **G** H I J K L M N O P Q R S T U V W X Y Z

group *noun*
groups

A **group** is a number of people or things that are together, or that belong together.
સમૂહ

grow *verb*
grows, growing, grew, grown

When something **grows**, it gets bigger.
વધવું

*The puppy **grew** into a huge dog.*

guess *verb*
guesses, guessing, guessed

If you **guess**, you say what you think is true about something, but you do not really know if you are right.
ધારવું

*Can you **guess** how old he is?*

guinea pig *noun*
guinea pigs

A **guinea pig** is a small animal with fur and no tail that people often keep as a pet.
ગીની પિગ, એક જાતનું પાલતુ પ્રાણી

guitar *noun*
guitars

A **guitar** is an instrument with strings that you play by pressing the strings with one hand and pulling them with the other hand.
ગિટાર

had
⇨ Look at **have**.
*We **had** a nice time.*

hadn't

Hadn't is short for **had not**.
નહોતું કર્યું
*I **hadn't** seen them for a long time.*

hair *noun*

Hair is the soft, fine threads that grow on your head and on the bodies of many animals.
વાળ
*I wash my **hair** every night.*

half *noun*
halves

A **half** is one of two equal parts that make up a whole thing.
અડધો ભાગ, અર્ધ
*We each had **half** of the cake.*

halves
⇨ Look at **half**.
*Cut the apples into **halves**.*

hamster *noun*
hamsters

A **hamster** is a small animal that looks like a fat mouse with a short tail. People often keep **hamsters** as pets.
ઉંદર જેવું એક નાનું પ્રાણી

hand noun
hands

Your **hands** are the parts of your body that are at the ends of your arms, and that you use to hold things. A **hand** has four fingers and a thumb.
હાથ

*I put my **hand** in my pocket and took out the letter.*

handle noun
handles

1 A **handle** is something that is joined to a door, a window, or a drawer, that you use to open and close it.
હાથો

*She pulled the **handle** of the drawer.*

2 A **handle** is also the part of something, for example a tool or a bag, that you use to hold it.
દંડો

*Hold the knife by its **handle**.*

hang verb
hangs, hanging, hung

If you **hang** something somewhere, you fix the top of it to something so that it does not touch the ground.
લટકવું, લટકાવવું

*She **hung** her coat on a peg.*

happen verb
happens, happening, happened

When something **happens**, it takes place.
બનવું કે થવું

*What's **happening** in the playground?*

happy adjective
happier, happiest

When you are **happy**, you feel pleased about something.
સુખ

hard adjective
harder, hardest

1 Something that is **hard** is solid, and it is not easy to bend it or break it.
કઠણ

*The glass broke on the **hard** floor.*

2 If something is **hard**, you have to try a lot to do it or to understand it.
મુશ્કેલ, અઘરું

*These sums are quite **hard**.*

has

⇒ Look at **have**.
*He **has** a sister.*

hasn't

Hasn't is short for **has not**.
(એણે) નથી કર્યું

*She **hasn't** anything to do.*

hat noun
hats

A **hat** is something that you can wear on your head.
ટોપી

hatch verb
hatches, hatching, hatched

When a baby bird or other animal **hatches**, it comes out of its egg by breaking the shell. You can also say that the egg **hatches**.
ઈંડામાંથી બચ્ચાંને બહાર કાઢવું

hate verb
hates, hating, hated

If you **hate** a person or a thing, you feel that you do not like them at all.
ધિક્કારવું, તિરસ્કારવું

*I **hate** onions.*

have verb
has, having, had

1 If you **have** something, it belongs to you.
હોવું

*Do you **have** any pets?*

2 When you **have** something, you feel it, or it happens to you.
થવું

*I **have** a bad cold.*

haven't

Haven't is short for **have not**.
(મેં / અમે) નથી કર્યું
*I **haven't** any chocolate left.*

hay *noun*

Hay is dry grass that is used to feed animals.
સૂકું ઘાસ

head *noun*
heads

1 Your **head** is the part of your body at the top that has your eyes, ears, nose, mouth, and brain in it.
માથું
*The ball hit him on the **head**.*

2 The **head** of something is the person who is its leader.
મુખ્ય શિક્ષક કે શિક્ષિકા
*He is the **head** of the school.*

heal *verb*
heals, healing, healed

If something like a broken bone **heals**, it gets better.
રૂઝાવું (ઘા કે ઈજા)

healthy *adjective*
healthier, healthiest

1 Someone who is **healthy** is well and strong and is not often ill.
તંદુરસ્ત
*People need exercise to stay **healthy**.*

2 Something that is **healthy** is good for you.
નીરોગી
*Eat **healthy** food like fruit and vegetables.*

hear *verb*
hears, hearing, heard

When you **hear** a sound, you notice it through your ears.
સાંભળવું
*I **heard** a dog barking.*

heart *noun*
hearts

Your **heart** is the part inside you that makes the blood move around your body.
હૃદય
*His **heart** was going fast.*

heavy *adjective*
heavier, heaviest

Something that is **heavy** weighs a lot.
વજનદાર
*This bag is very **heavy**.*

he'd

1 **He'd** is short for **he had**.
એણે
He'd seen it before.

2 **He'd** is also short for **he would**.
એણે
He'd like them.

hedge *noun*
hedges

A **hedge** is a row of bushes growing close together that makes a kind of wall. You often see **hedges** around fields.
ઝાંખરાની વાડ

heel *noun*
heels

Your **heels** are the parts of your feet at the back, below your ankles.
એડી
*He dragged his **heels** along the ground.*

height *noun*
heights

Your **height** is how tall you are.
ઊંચાઈ
*We all measured our **heights**.*

held

⇒ Look at **hold**.

*Mum **held** my hand as we crossed the road.*

helicopter *noun*
helicopters

A **helicopter** is a small aircraft with long blades on top that go round very quickly. **Helicopters** can fly straight up and down and stay in one place in the air.
હેલીકૉપ્ટર

he'll

He'll is short for **he will**.
તે કરશે (પુલ્લિંગ)

***He'll** come back soon.*

hello

You say **hello** to someone when you meet them.
કેમ છો!

help *verb*
helps, helping, helped

If you **help** someone, you make it easier for them to do something.
મદદ

*He **helped** me with my homework.*

hen *noun*
hens

A **hen** is a chicken that is a female. People often eat **hens'** eggs as food.
મરઘી, કૂકડી

her

You use **her** to talk about a woman or a girl, or to say that something belongs to a woman or a girl.
તે, તેની (સ્ત્રીલિંગ)

*I gave **her** back **her** pen.*

herd *noun*
herds

A **herd** is a large group of animals that lives together.
જાનવરોનું ટોળું, ધણ

*We saw a **herd** of deer in the forest.*

here

Here means the place where you are.
અહીં, આ જગ્યાએ,

*Come and sit **here**.*

hers

You use **hers** to say that something belongs to a woman or a girl.
તેણીનું

*She said that the bag was **hers**.*

herself

You use **herself** when you want to say that something a woman or a girl does has an effect on her.
તેણી પોતે

*She pulled **herself** out of the water.*

he's

He's is short for **he is**.
એ છે (પુલ્લિંગ)

***He's** six years old.*

hexagon *noun*
hexagons

A **hexagon** is a shape with six straight sides.
ષટ્કોણ, ષડ્ભુજ

hid

⇒ Look at **hide**.

*They **hid** in the cupboard.*

a b c d e f g h i j k l m n o p q r s t u v w x y z

hidden

⇨ Look at **hide**.

*He was **hidden** under the bed.*

hide *verb*
hides, hiding, hid, hidden

1 If you **hide** something, you put it where no one can see it or find it.
સંતાડવું
*He **hid** his bike behind the wall.*

2 If you **hide** what you feel, you do not let people know about it.
છાનું રાખવું કે છુપાવવું
*She tried to **hide** how angry she was.*

high *adjective*
higher, highest

1 Something that is **high** is tall or is a long way above the ground.
ઊંચું
*There was a **high** wall around the house.*

2 **High** also means great in amount or strength.
વધારે
*They charged us a **high** price.*

3 A **high** sound or voice goes up a long way.
તીવ્ર
*She spoke in a **high** voice.*

hill *noun*
hills

A **hill** is a piece of land that is higher than the land around it. **Hills** are not as high as mountains.
નાની ટેકરી

him

You use **him** to talk about a man or a boy.
તેને
*We met **him** at the station.*

himself

You use **himself** when you want to say that something a man or a boy does has an effect on him.
તેઓ પોતે
*He fell and hurt **himself**.*

hippopotamus *noun*
hippopotamuses *or* hippopotami

A **hippopotamus** is a large animal with short legs and thick skin that lives near rivers.
જળઘોડો, હિપોપોટેમસ, જાડી ચામડીવાળું જળચર પ્રાણી

his

You use **his** to say that something belongs to a man or a boy.
તેનું (પુલ્લિંગ)
*He showed me **his** new football.*

history *noun*

History is the story of what has happened in the past.
ઇતિહાસ

hit *verb*
hits, hitting, hit

If you **hit** something, you touch it with a lot of strength.
ફટકો મારવો, મારવું
*She **hit** the ball with the bat.*

hive *noun*
hives

A **hive** is a place where bees live.
મધપૂડો

hold *verb*
holds, holding, held

1 When you **hold** something, you have it in your hands or your arms.
પકડવું, પકડી રાખવું
*She **held** the baby in her arms.*

2 If something **holds** an amount of something, then that is how much it has room for inside.
સમાવવાની ક્ષમતા હોવી
*The theatre **holds** 400 people.*

hole *noun*
holes

A **hole** is a gap or a hollow place in something.
કાણું
*We dug a **hole** in the ground.*

holiday *noun*
holidays

A **holiday** is a time when you do not need to work or go to school.
રજાનો કે ઉજાણીનો દિવસ

hollow *adjective*

Something that is **hollow** has an empty space inside it.
પોલું
*The owl's nest was in a **hollow** tree.*

home *noun*
homes

Your **home** is the place where you live.
ઘર
*We stayed at **home** and watched TV.*

homework *noun*

Homework is something like sums that a teacher gives you to work on at home.
ગૃહકાર્ય

honest *adjective*

If someone is **honest**, they do not tell lies, and you can believe what they say.
પ્રમાણિક

honey *noun*

Honey is a sweet, very thick liquid that is made by bees. You can eat **honey** on bread.
મધ

hoof *noun*
hooves

A **hoof** is the hard part of a horse's foot. Deer and cows also have **hooves**.
જાનવરના પગની ખરી

hop *verb*
hops, hopping, hopped

1 If you **hop**, you jump on one foot.
કૂદકો મારવો

2 When animals or birds **hop**, they jump with two feet together.
(જાનવરનું) ચારે પગે ઊલળવું

hope *verb*
hopes, hoping, hoped

If you **hope** that something will happen, you want it to happen.
આશા કે ઈચ્છા રાખવી
*I **hope** you feel better soon.*

horn *noun*
horns

1 A **horn** is one of the hard bones with sharp points that grow out of some animals' heads. Goats and bulls have **horns**.
શિંગડું

2 A **horn** is also an instrument that you blow into to make music.
પીતળનું એક સુષિર

horrible *adjective*

If something is **horrible**, it is very nasty.
ભયંકર
*There was a **horrible** smell.*

a b c d e f g h i j k l m n o p q r s t u v w x y z

A B C D E F G H I J K L M N O P Q R S T U V W X Y Z

horse *noun*
horses

A **horse** is a large animal with a long tail and four legs. People ride on **horses** or use them to pull things along.
ઘોડો

hospital *noun*
hospitals

A **hospital** is a building where doctors and nurses care for people who are ill or hurt.
મોટું દવાખાનું - ઈસ્પિતાલ

hot *adjective*
hotter, hottest

If something is **hot**, it is very warm.
ગરમ

*Don't touch the plate – it's **hot**.*

hour *noun*
hours

An **hour** is used for measuring time. There are sixty minutes in an **hour**, and twenty-four **hours** in a day.
કલાક

house *noun*
houses

A **house** is a building where people live.
ઘર

*Come to my **house** for dinner.*

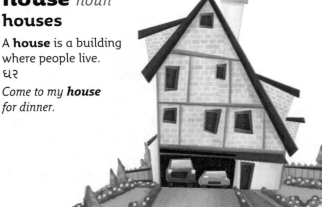

how

1 You use the word **how** when you ask about the way that something happens or the way that you do something.
કેવી રીતે, કેમ (કરીને)

*   ***How** do you spell your name?*

2 You also use **how** when you ask about an amount.
કેટલું, કેટલાં

*   ***How** many people were at the party?*

hug *verb*
hugs, hugging, hugged

When you **hug** someone, you put your arms around them and hold them close to you.
જોરથી ભેટવું, છાતીસરસું ચાંપવું

*She **hugged** me as we said goodbye.*

huge *adjective*

Something that is **huge** is very big.
વિશાળ

*Elephants are **huge** animals.*

human *adjective*

Something that is **human** is to do with people, and not animals or machines.
માનવી

*There are over 200 bones in the **human** body.*

hundred *noun*

A **hundred** is the number 100.
સો

hung

⇨ Look at **hang**.
*He **hung** from the bars.*

hungry *adjective*
hungrier, hungriest

If you are **hungry**, you want to eat something.
ભૂખ્યું

hunt *verb*
hunts, hunting, hunted

1 When animals **hunt**, they chase another animal to kill it for food.
શિકાર કરવો

*The lions **hunted** a zebra.*

2 If you **hunt** for something, you try to find it.
શોધવું

*I **hunted** for my keys.*

hurry *verb*
hurries, hurrying, hurried

If you **hurry**, you move quickly or do something quickly.
ઉતાવળ કે ઝડપ કરવી

*We'll be late if we don't **hurry**.*

hurt *verb*
hurts, hurting, hurt

If you **hurt** someone or something, you make them feel pain.
ઈજા કરવી

*I fell over and **hurt** my leg yesterday.*

husband *noun*
husbands

A woman's **husband** is the man she is married to.
પતિ

hut *noun*
huts

A **hut** is a small building with one or two rooms. **Huts** are made of wood, mud, or grass.
ઝૂંપડી

hutch *noun*
hutches

A **hutch** is a kind of cage made of wood and wire, where people keep rabbits and other small pets.
સસલાં ઇ. માટે પેટી કે ખોખાં જેવું ઘર

I

You use **I** to talk about yourself.
હું

I like chocolate.

ice *noun*

Ice is water that has frozen. It is very cold and hard.
બરફ

*The ground was covered with **ice**.*

ice cream *noun*

Ice cream is a very cold, sweet food that is made from frozen milk or cream.
આઇસક્રીમ

icicle *noun*
icicles

An **icicle** is a long piece of ice with a point at the end that hangs down from something. **Icicles** are made from dripping water that has frozen.
નેવે લટકતો બરફનો લોલક જેવો ટુકડો

I'd

1 **I'd** is short for **I had**.
મેં કર્યું હતું
I'd been there before.

2 **I'd** is also short for **I would**.
હું કરીશ
I'd like to go to the zoo.

a
b
c
d
e
f
g
h
i
j
k
l
m
n
o
p
q
r
s
t
u
v
w
x
y
z

idea *noun*
ideas

An **idea** is something new that you have thought of.
વિચાર
*He had an **idea** for a story.*

ill *adjective*

When you are **ill**,
you do not feel well.
બીમાર
*She is too **ill** to go to school.*

I'll

I'll is short for **I will**.
હું કરીશ
I'll come back tomorrow.

illness *noun*
illnesses

If you have an **illness**, you do not feel well.
માંદગી
*He has just had a very bad **illness**.*

I'm

I'm is short for **I am**.
હું છું
I'm hungry.

imagine *verb*
imagines, imagining, imagined

If you **imagine** something, you make a picture of it in your mind.
કલ્પના કરવી
Imagine that you are a cat.

immediately

If you do something **immediately**, you do it now.
તરત જ
*Stop that noise **immediately**!*

important *adjective*

1   If something is **important**, people care about it and think about it a lot.
મહત્વનું, અગત્યનું
*It is **important** not to tell lies.*

2   If someone is **important**, people pay a lot of attention to what they say and do.
મોભાદાર, પ્રભાવશીલ,
*She is a very **important** person.*

impossible *adjective*

If something is **impossible**, it cannot be done, or it cannot happen.
અસંભવ
*It is **impossible** to see in the dark.*

in

1   **In** means not outside.
-માં, અંદર
*The juice is **in** the fridge.*

2   You also use **in** to say when something happens.
(અવધિ) દરમ્યાન
*He was born **in** March.*

inch *noun*
inches

An **inch** is used for measuring the length of something. There are about two and half centimetres in an **inch**.
ઇંચ

indoors

If you are **indoors**, you are inside a building.
ઘરની અંદર

information *noun*

Information about something is facts that tell you about it.
જાણકારી, ખબર
*I need some **information** about birds.*

ink noun

Ink is a liquid that you use to write or print with. Pens have **ink** inside them.
શાહી

insect noun
insects

An **insect** is a small animal with six legs, for example a bee or a beetle.
Many **insects** have wings and can fly.
જીવાણુ

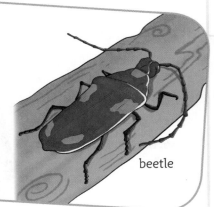

beetle

inside

1 If something is **inside** another thing, it is in it.
અંદર
*There was a letter **inside** the envelope.*

2 **Inside** also means indoors.
અંદરની બાજુ
*He went **inside** and locked the door.*

instructions noun

Instructions are words or pictures that tell you how to do something.
સૂચનાઓ
*Here are the **instructions** for building the tent.*

instrument noun
instruments

1 An **instrument** is a tool that you use to do something.
સાધન, ઓજાર, હથિયાર
*The doctor used an **instrument** to look in my ears.*

2 An **instrument** is also something, for example a piano or a guitar, that you use to make music.
સંગીતનું વાદ્ય કે વાજું
*He plays three **instruments**.*

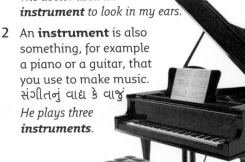

intelligent adjective

If a person is **intelligent**, they are able to understand and learn things quickly.
બુદ્ધિમાન

interesting adjective

If something is **interesting**, you want to know more about it.
મનોરંજક, રસિક, ચિત્તાકર્ષક

Internet noun

The **Internet** is something that joins a computer to other computers all over the world. You send emails using the **Internet**.
ઇંટરનેટ, આંતરરાષ્ટ્રીય કમ્પ્યૂટરતંત્ર

interrupt verb
interrupts, interrupting, interrupted

If you **interrupt** someone, you say or do something that makes them stop in the middle of what they are doing.
વિક્ષેપ નાખવો
*Don't **interrupt** the teacher when she's talking.*

invention noun
inventions

An **invention** is something that someone has made, and that nobody has ever thought of or made before.
નવસર્જન, શોધ
*His new **invention** is a car that can fly.*

invisible adjective

If something is **invisible**, you cannot see it.
અદૃશ્ય

invite verb
invites, inviting, invited

If you **invite** someone to something, for example a party, you ask them to come to it.
આમંત્રણ આપવું, નોતરવું

a
b
c
d
e
f
g
h
i
j
k
l
m
n
o
p
q
r
s
t
u
v
w
x
y
z

A
B
C
D
E
F
G
H
I
J
K
L
M
N
O
P
Q
R
S
T
U
V
W
X
Y
Z

iron *noun*
irons

1 **Iron** is a strong, hard, grey metal.
લોખંડ, લોઢું

2 An **iron** is a piece of equipment with a flat bottom that gets hot. You move the bottom over clothes to make them smooth.
ઈસ્ત્રી

is

➡ Look at **be**.
She is six years old.

island *noun*
islands

An **island** is a piece of land that has water all around it.
ટાપુ

isn't

Isn't is short for **is not**.
નથી
He isn't very happy.

it

You use **it** to talk about a thing or an animal.
તે
This is a good book – have you read it?

its

You use **its** to say that something belongs to a thing or an animal.
તેનું, તેની, તેનો
The lion lifted its head.

it's

It's is short for **it is**.
એ છે
It's one o'clock.

I've

I've is short for **I have**.
મારી પાસે છે
I've been playing football.

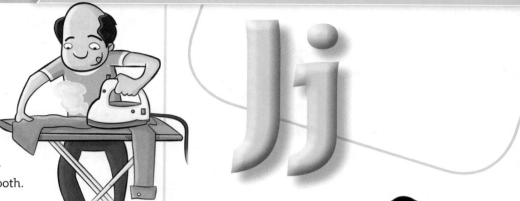

jacket *noun*
jackets

A **jacket** is a short coat.
જાડું ઉપવસ્ત્ર

jam *noun*

Jam is a soft, sweet food that is made from fruit and sugar.
મુરબ્બો
I love strawberry jam on my bread.

January *noun*

January is the month after December and before February. It has 31 days.
વર્ષનો પહેલો મહિનો, જૅન્યુઅરી

jar *noun*
jars

A **jar** is a glass container with a lid that is used for storing food.
બરણી
Make sure you put the lid back on the jar.

jaw *noun*
jaws

Your **jaws** are the top and bottom bones of your mouth.
જડબું

jaw

jeans *noun*

Jeans are blue trousers with pockets at the front and back.
જીન્સ
*Everyone on the trip wore **jeans** and a bright T-shirt.*

jelly *noun*

Jelly is a clear, sweet food that is solid but soft.
જેલી - મુરબ્બા જેવી વાનગી
*We had birthday cake, then **jelly** and ice cream.*

jet *noun*
jets

A **jet** is a plane that flies very fast.
જેટ વિમાન

jewel *noun*
jewels

1 A **jewel** is a valuable stone, like a diamond.
રત્ન, મણિ

2 **Jewels** are things made with valuable stones, that you wear to decorate your body.
રત્નજડિત ઘરેણું
*She put the **jewels** in the box and turned the key.*

jigsaw *noun*
jigsaws

A **jigsaw** is a picture on cardboard that has been cut up into pieces. You have to fit them together again.
પૂંઠા અથવા લાકડાના પાટિયા પર દોરેલા ચિત્રના આડાઅવળા કાપેલા ટુકડાને જોડવાનો એક પ્રકારનો કોયડો
*The children put the last pieces in the **jigsaw**.*

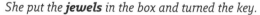

job *noun*
jobs

A **job** is the work that a person does to earn money.
કામ
*My sister wants to get a **job**.*

join *verb*
joins, joining, joined

1 If you **join** a group of people, you become one of the group.
બીજાની સાથે જોડાવું
*Come and **join** the music group after school on Mondays.*

2 When things **join**, or you **join** them, they come together.
જોડવું, સાંધવું
*They **joined** hands and danced.*

joke *noun*
jokes

A **joke** is something that someone says to make you laugh.
વિનોદનો ટૂચકો, ગમ્મત
*Grandfather always tells us **jokes** after dinner.*

journey *noun*
journeys

When you make a **journey**, you travel from one place to another.
યાત્રા
*It was a difficult **journey** that took several days.*

jug *noun*
jugs

A **jug** is a container with a handle. You use a **jug** for pouring liquids.
કુંજો, ચંબુ
*There is a **jug** of cold water on the table.*

juice *noun*
juices

Juice is the liquid from a fruit or vegetable.
રસ
*He had a large glass of fresh orange **juice**.*

a b c d e f g h i **j** k l m n o p q r s t u v w x y z

A
B
C
D
E
F
G
H
I
J
K
L
M
N
O
P
Q
R
S
T
U
V
W
X
Y
Z

July noun

July is the month after June and before August. It has 31 days.
વર્ષનો સાતમો મહિનો, જુલાઈ

jump verb
jumps, jumping, jumped

When you **jump**, you bend your knees and push yourself into the air.
છલાંગ કે ફૂદકો મારવો
*I **jumped** over the fence.*

jumper noun
jumpers

You wear a **jumper** to keep yourself warm. It has sleeves and covers the top half of your body.
શરીરપર પહેરવાનું લાંબી બાંયનું ગૂંથેલું વસ્ત્ર

June noun

June is the month after May and before July. It has 30 days.
વર્ષનો છઠ્ઠો મહિનો, જૂન

jungle noun
jungles

A **jungle** is a thick, wet forest in a hot country.
જંગલ, વન
*They followed the path deep into the **jungle**.*

just

If you **just** did something, you did it a very short time ago.
અબઘડી, હમણાં જ
*We **just** got home after an awful journey.*

kangaroo noun
kangaroos

A **kangaroo** is a large Australian animal that carries its babies in a pocket on its stomach.
કાંગારુ

keen adjective
keener, keenest

If you are **keen**, you want to do something very much.
ઉત્સાહી, આતુર
*Everyone was **keen** to help.*

keep verb
keeps, keeping, kept

1 If someone **keeps** away from a place, they do not go near it.
રહેવું
Keep away from the road.

2 If someone **keeps** still or warm, they stay like that.
કોઈ હાલતમાં ટકી રહેવું
*We lit a fire to **keep** warm.*
"Keep still!"

3 If you **keep** doing something, you do it many times or you do it some more.
ચાલુ રાખવું
*I **keep** forgetting to take my umbrella.*

4 When you **keep** something, you store it somewhere.
સાચવી રાખવું
*She **kept** her money under the bed.*

kennel noun
kennels

A **kennel** is a small house where a dog can sleep.
કૂતરાનું ઘર

kept

⇨ Look at **keep**.
*She **kept** her head down.*

kettle *noun*
kettles

A **kettle** is a metal container with a lid and a handle, that you use for boiling water.
કીટલી

*Mum put the **kettle** on and made some tea.*

key *noun*
keys

1 A **key** is a piece of metal that opens or closes a lock.
ચાવી
*They put the **key** in the door and it opened.*

2 The **keys** on a computer or instrument are the buttons that you press on it.
બટન
*Press the "Enter" **key**.*

kick *verb*
kicks, kicking, kicked

If you **kick** something, you hit it with your foot.
લાત મારવી
*He **kicked** the ball really hard.*

kid *noun*
kids

A **kid** is a child.
બાળક
*They have three **kids**.*

kill *verb*
kills, killing, killed

To **kill** a living thing is to make it die.
હત્યા કરવી
*The earthquake **killed** 62 people.*

kilogram *noun*
kilograms

A **kilogram** is used for measuring how heavy things are. There are 1,000 grams in a **kilogram**.
વજનનું એક માપ, કિલોગ્રામ
*The box weighs 4.5 **kilograms**.*

kilometre *noun*
kilometres

A **kilometre** is used for measuring distance. There are 1,000 metres in a **kilometre**, which is about 0.62 miles.
કિલોમીટર, અંતરનું એક માપ (1000 મીટર)

kind *noun*
kinds

A **kind** of thing is a type or sort of that thing.
વર્ગ, પ્રકાર, જાતિ
*What **kind** of car is that?*

kind *adjective*
kinder, kindest

Someone who is **kind** is friendly and helps you.
દયાળુ, કૃપાળુ, માયાળુ
*Thank you for being so **kind** to me.*

king *noun*
kings

A **king** is a man who rules a country.
રાજા
*We saw the **king** and queen arriving.*

kiss *verb*
kisses, kissing, kissed

If you **kiss** someone, you touch them with your lips.
ચુંબન
*We **kissed** goodbye at the airport.*

kitchen *noun*
kitchens

A **kitchen** is a room that is used for cooking.
રસોઈઘર

a
b
c
d
e
f
g
h
i
j
k
l
m
n
o
p
q
r
s
t
u
v
w
x
y
z

A
B
C
D
E
F
G
H
I
J
K
L
M
N
O
P
Q
R
S
T
U
V
W
X
Y
Z

kite noun
kites

A **kite** is a toy that you fly in the wind at the end of a long string.
પતંગ
*We went to the beach to fly **kites**.*

kitten noun
kittens

A **kitten** is a very young cat.
બિલાડીનું બચ્ચું

knee noun
knees

Your **knee** is the part in the middle of your leg where it bends.
ઘૂંટણ
*I fell over and hurt my **knee**.*

kneel verb
kneels, kneeling, knelt

When you **kneel**, you bend your legs and rest on one or both of your knees.
ઘૂંટણિયે પડવું, નમવું
*She **knelt** down beside the bed.*

knew
⇨ Look at **know**.
*I **knew** all the kids at the party.*

knife noun
knives

A **knife** is a sharp metal tool that you use to cut things.
છરી, છરો, ઇત્યાદિ જેવું કાપવાનું ઓજાર
*I finished and put down my **knife** and fork.*

knight noun
knights

In the past, a **knight** was a soldier who rode a horse.
શૂરવીર યોદ્ધો

knit verb
knits, knitting, knitted

If you **knit** something, you make it from a long piece of wool by using two special sticks.
ગૂંથવું
*My grandmother sat **knitting**.*

knives
⇨ Look at **knife**.
*We put all the **knives** away in their box.*

knock verb
knocks, knocking, knocked

If you **knock** on something, you hit it to make a noise.
ખખડાવવું
*She went to his house and **knocked** on the door.*

knot noun
knots

You make a **knot** when you tie two pieces of something together.
ગાંઠ
*He picked up the rope and tied a **knot** in it.*

know verb
knows, knowing, knew, known

1 If you **know** something, you have that information in your mind.
જાણવું
*You should **know** the answer to that question.*

2 If you **know** a person, you have met them and spoken to them.
ઓળખવું
*I didn't **know** any of the other people in the class.*

L l

label *noun*
labels

A **label** is a small note on something that gives you information about it.
વસ્તુ ઉપર ચોઢેલી ચિઠ્ઠી કે કાપલી
*The prices are on the **labels**.*

lace *noun*
laces

1 **Lace** is a pretty cloth that has patterns of holes in it.
કોર, કસબની કોર
*Her dress was dark blue with a white **lace** collar.*

2 **Laces** are like pieces of string for fastening shoes.
જોડા ઇ.ની નાડી, દોરી
*He put on his shoes and tied the **laces**.*

ladder *noun*
ladders

A **ladder** is a set of steps that you can move around. You use it for reaching high places.
સીડી
*He climbed the **ladder** to see over the wall.*

lady *noun*
ladies

You can use **lady** to talk about a woman in a polite way.
મહિલા
*She's a very nice old **lady**.*

ladybird *noun*
ladybirds

A **ladybird** is a small round beetle that has red wings with black spots.
કાળા ટપકાંવાળું બહુધા રાતા બદામી રંગનું એક જાતનું વાંદાના વર્ગનું જીવડું

laid
⇨ Look at **lay**.
*She **laid** out the food on the table.*

lain
⇨ Look at **lie**.
*He had **lain** awake all night, worrying.*

lake *noun*
lakes

A **lake** is an area of water with land around it.
તળાવ

lamb *noun*
lambs

A **lamb** is a young sheep.
ઘેટાનું બચ્ચું

lamp *noun*
lamps

A **lamp** is a light that uses electricity, oil or gas.
દીપક
*She turned on the **lamp** by her bed.*

land *noun*

Land is an area of ground.
જમીન, ભૂમિ
*This is good farm **land**.*

land *verb*
lands, landing, landed

When something **lands**, it comes down to the ground after moving through the air.
નીચે ઉતરવું
*The ball **landed** in the middle of the road.*

lane *noun*
lanes

A **lane** is a narrow road, usually in the country.
સાંકડો રસ્તો, શેરી, ગલી

a
b
c
d
e
f
g
h
i
j
k
l
m
n
o
p
q
r
s
t
u
v
w
x
y
z

language *noun*
languages

A **language** is a set of words that the people of a country use in talking or writing.
ભાષા
*The English **language** has over 500,000 words.*

lap *noun*
laps

Your **lap** is the flat area on top of your thighs when you are sitting down.
ખોળો
*The boy sat on his dad's **lap**.*

large *adjective*
larger, largest

A **large** thing or person is big or bigger than usual.
વિશાળ, વિસ્તીર્ણ, વ્યાપક, કદાવર
*This fish lives in **large** rivers and lakes.*

last *adjective*

1 The **last** thing is the one before this one.
આ સમય અગાઉનું
*In the **last** lesson, we looked at some flowers.*

2 The **last** thing or person comes after all the others.
આખરી, છેવટનું
*I read the **last** three pages of the chapter.*

late
later, latest

1 **Late** means near the end of a period of time.
નિયત કે હમેશના સમય પછીનું
*It was **late** in the afternoon.*

2 **Late** also means after the proper time.
મોડું
*We arrived **late** for our class.*

laugh *verb*
laughs, laughing, laughed

When you **laugh**, you smile and make a sound because something is funny.
હસવું, દાંત કાઢવા
*The boys all **laughed** at his joke.*

law *noun*
laws

A **law** is a rule that tells people what they may or may not do in a country.
કાયદો

lawn *noun*
lawns

A **lawn** is an area of short grass.
વ્યવસ્થિતપણે કાતરેલા ઘાસવાળી જમીન
*Let's sit on the **lawn**.*

lay *verb*
lays, laying, laid

1 When you **lay** something somewhere, you put it down so that it lies there.
મૂકવું, રાખવું
***Lay** the dishes on the table.*

2 When a bird **lays** an egg, it pushes an egg out of its body.
ઈંડું સેવવું

lay

⇨ Look at **lie**.
*We **lay** on the grass and looked at the sky.*

layer *noun*
layers

A **layer** is something that covers a surface, or that lies between two other things.
સ્તર
*A **layer** of new snow covered the street.*

lazy *adjective*
lazier, laziest

A **lazy** person does not like working.
આળસુ
*He was too **lazy** to read the whole book.*

lead *verb*
leads, leading, led

If you **lead** someone to a place, you take them there.
દોરવું, રસ્તો બતાવવો
*I took his hand and started to **lead** him into the house.*

lead *noun*

If you are in the **lead** in a race or competition, you are winning.
–માં પ્રથમ સ્થાન હોવું, અગ્રેસર થવું
*Our team was in the **lead** after ten minutes.*

lead *noun*

Lead is a soft, grey, heavy metal.
સીસું

leader *noun*

leaders

The **leader** of a group of people or a country is the person who is in charge of it.
નેતા
*Your team **leaders** have your instructions.*

leaf *noun*

leaves

The **leaves** of a plant are the parts that are flat, thin, and usually green.
પાંદડું
*A dry, brown **leaf** floated on the water.*

lean *verb*

leans, leaning, leant or **leaned**

When you **lean**, you bend your body from your waist.
નમવું, વળવું
*She **leant** forwards and looked at me again.*

leap *verb*

leaps, leaping, leapt or **leaped**

If you **leap**, you jump a long way or very high.
કૂદવું, ઉછળવું, છલાંગ મારવી
*He **leaped** in the air and waved his hands.*

learn *verb*

learns, learning, learnt or **learned**

When you **learn** something, you get to know it or how to do it.
શીખવું
*When did you **learn** to swim?*

leather *noun*

Leather is the skin of some animals that you can use for making things.
ચામડું
*Is your jacket made of real **leather**?*

leave *verb*

leaves, leaving, left

1 When you **leave** a place, you go away from it.
–થી જતા રહેવું, છોડીને જવું
*Our bus **leaves** in an hour.*

2 If you **leave** something somewhere, you do not bring it with you.
છોડવું, પડતું મૂકવું
*I **left** my bags in the car.*

leaves

⇨ Look at **leaf**.
*The **leaves** are beginning to turn brown.*

led

⇨ Look at **lead**.
*The woman **led** me through the door into her office.*

left *noun*

The **left** is one side of something. For example, on a page, English writing begins on the **left**.
ડાબી બાજુ
*The school is on the **left** at the end of the road.*

left

⇨ Look at **leave**.
*The teacher suddenly **left** the room.*

a
b
c
d
e
f
g
h
i
j
k
l
m
n
o
p
q
r
s
t
u
v
w
x
y
z

A
B
C
D
E
F
G
H
I
J
K
L
M
N
O
P
Q
R
S
T
U
V
W
X
Y
Z

leg *noun*
legs

1 A person's or animal's **legs** are the long parts of their body that they use for walking and standing.
પગ, ટાંટિયો
*Stand with your arms stretched out and your **legs** apart.*

2 The **legs** of a table or chair are the long parts that it stands on.
ખુરશી ઈ.નો પાયો
*One of the **legs** is loose.*

leg

lemon *noun*
lemons

A **lemon** is a yellow fruit with very sour juice.
લીંબુ

lend *verb*
lends, lending, lent

If you **lend** someone something, you give it to them for a period of time and then they give it back to you.
ઉછીનું આપવું, (પૈસા ઇ.)
*Will you **lend** me your pen?*

length *noun*
lengths

The **length** of something is how long it is from one end to the other.
લંબાઈ
*The table is about a metre in **length**.*

lent

⇨ Look at **lend**.
*I **lent** her two books to read on holiday.*

leopard *noun*
leopards

A **leopard** is a large, wild cat. **Leopards** have yellow fur with black spots, and live in Africa and Asia.
દીપડો

less *adjective*

Less means a smaller amount.
ઓછું, ઓછા પ્રમાણમાં
*I am trying to spend **less** money on sweets.*

lesson *noun*
lessons

A **lesson** is a period of time when someone teaches you something.
પાઠ
*My sister has a piano **lesson** every Monday.*

let *verb*
lets, letting, let

1 If you **let** someone do something, you allow them to do it.
રજા કે છૂટ આપવી

2 You can say **let's** when you want someone to do something with you. **Let's** is short for **let us**.
તજવું, જતું કરવું
Let's go!

letter *noun*
letters

1 A **letter** is a message on paper that you post to someone.
પત્ર
*I received a **letter** from a friend.*

2 **Letters** are shapes that you write to make words.
અક્ષર
*The children practised writing the **letters** in class.*

lettuce *noun*
lettuces

A **lettuce** is a vegetable with large green leaves that you eat in salads.
આછાં લીલા પાંદડાવાળો એક વિલાયતી છોડ (જે ખવાય)

library *noun*
libraries

A **library** is a place where you can go to read or borrow books.
પુસ્તકાલય
*I'm going to the **library** to look for a book about whales.*

lick *verb*
licks, licking, licked

If you **lick** something, you move your tongue over it.
ચાટવું
Lick the stamp before you put it on the envelope.

lid noun
lids

A **lid** is the top of a container that you can remove.
પાત્રનું ઢાંકણું
She lifted the lid of the box.

lie verb
lies, lying, lay, lain

When you **lie** somewhere, your body is flat, and you are not standing or sitting.
સૂવું, આડા થવું
Lie on the bed and close your eyes for a while.

lie noun
lies

A **lie** is something you say that is not true.
જૂઠું બોલવું
You told me a lie!

life noun
lives

Your **life** is the period of time when you are alive.
જીવન
I want to live here for the rest of my life.

lift verb
lifts, lifting, lifted

When you **lift** something, you take it and move it up.
ઊંચકવું, ઉપર લેવું
He lifted the bag on to his shoulder.

light noun
lights

1 **Light** is the bright energy that comes from the sun, that lets you see things.
અજવાળું
A little light comes into the room through the thin curtains.

2 A **light** is something like a lamp, that allows you to see.
અજવાળાનું ઉદ્‌ગમસ્થાન
There was only one small light in the room.

light adjective
lighter, lightest

1 If a place is **light**, it is bright because of the sun or lamps.
ઊજળું
It gets light at about 6 o'clock here.

2 Something that is **light** is not heavy.
હળવું; ફીરું
The chair is quite light so we can move it if we want to.

3 A **light** colour is pale.
આંખુ
His shirt was light blue.

light verb
lights, lighting, lit

When you **light** a fire, it starts burning.
પેટવવું, ચેતાવવું
We used a whole box of matches to light the fire.

lightning noun

Lightning is the very bright flashes of light in the sky in a storm.
આકાશી વીજળી
There was thunder and lightning and big black clouds in the sky.

like

1 If things or people are **like** each other, they are almost the same.
(બીજા)ના જેવું, સરખું, સમાન
He's very funny, like my uncle.

2 You say what something or someone is **like** when you are talking about how they seem to you.
જાણે કે, કેમ જાણે
"What was the party like?"—"Oh it was great!"

like verb
likes, liking, liked

If you **like** something, you think it is nice or interesting.
ગમવું, પસંદ પડવું
Do you like swimming?

line noun
lines

A **line** is a long, thin mark or shape.
રેખા, લીટી
*Draw a **line** at the bottom of the page.*

lion noun
lions

A **lion** is a large wild cat that lives in Africa. **Lions** have yellow fur, and male **lions** have long hair on their head and neck.
સિંહ

lip noun
lips

Your **lips** are the edges of your mouth.
હોઠ
*He bit his **lip**.*

liquid noun
liquids

A **liquid** is something that you can pour. Water and oil are **liquids**.
પ્રવાહી
*The bottle is full of clear **liquid**.*

list noun
lists

A **list** is a set of names or other things that you write one below the other.
વસ્તુઓ, નામો ઇ.ની યાદી, સૂચિ
*There are six names on the **list**.*

listen verb
listens, listening, listened

If you **listen** to something, you hear it and give it your attention.
સાંભળવું
*He's **listening** to the radio.*

lit
➡ Look at **light**.
*He took a match and **lit** the candle.*

litre noun
litres

A **litre** is used for measuring liquid.
મૅટ્રિક પદ્ધતિનું પ્રવાહી એક માપ, પરિમાણ

litter noun
Litter is rubbish that people drop in the street.
કચરો
*Please don't drop any **litter**.*

little adjective
littler, littlest

A person or thing that is **little** is small in size.
માપ, કદ, વિસ્તાર, સંખ્યા કે મહત્વની દૃષ્ટિએ ઓછું કે થોડું
*They live in a **little** house.*

live verb
lives, living, lived

1 You **live** in the place where your home is.
રહેવું
*Where do you **live**?*

2 To **live** means to be alive.
જીવન જીવવું
*We all need water to **live**.*

lives
➡ Look at **life**.
*Their **lives** were changed.*

lizard noun
lizards

A **lizard** is a small reptile with a long tail and rough skin.
કાચિંડો, સરડો (૨) ગરોળી

load verb
loads, loading, loaded

If you **load** a vehicle, you put something on it.
ભાર મૂકવું
*We finished **loading** the bags on to the lorry.*

loaf noun
loaves

A **loaf** is bread that you cut into slices.
પાઉંરોટી
*He bought a **loaf** of bread and some cheese.*

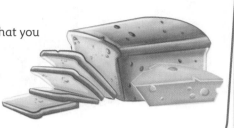

lock verb
locks, locking, locked

When you **lock** a door, you close it with a key.
તાળું મારવું કે મારીને બંધ કરવું
*Are you sure you **locked** the front door?*

log noun
logs

A **log** is a thick piece of wood from a tree.
લાકડાનું ઢીમચું
*We sat around a **log** fire.*

lolly noun
lollies

A **lolly** is a sweet or ice cream on a stick.
લોલી-લૉલીપપ, નાની સળી પર બેસાડેલું મીઠાઈનું ચકતું

long adjective
longer, longest

1 Something that is **long** takes a lot of time.
લાંબું
*The afternoon lessons seemed very **long**.*

2 Something that is **long** measures a great distance from one end to the other.
લાંબું, લંબાવેલા આકારનું
*There is a **long** table in the middle of the kitchen.*

look verb
looks, looking, looked

1 When you **look** at something, you turn your eyes so that you can see it.
જોવું
*I **looked** at the clock and yawned.*

2 You use **look** when you describe how a person seems.
દેખાવું
*The little girl **looked** sad.*

loose adjective
looser, loosest

1 Something that is **loose** moves when it should not.
ઢીલું
*One of the table legs is **loose**.*

2 **Loose** clothes are rather large and are not tight.
મોકળું
*Wear **loose**, comfortable clothes when you do the exercises.*

lorry noun
lorries

A **lorry** is a large vehicle for moving things by road.
ભારવાહક મોટર ખટારો

lose verb
loses, losing, lost

1 If you **lose** a game, you do not win it.
હારવું
*Our team **lost** the match by one point.*

2 If you **lose** something, you do not know where it is.
ગુમાવવું
*I've **lost** my keys.*

lost adjective

If you are **lost**, you do not know where you are.
ખોવાયેલું, નષ્ટ, ગુમ કે લુપ્ત થયેલું
*I suddenly knew that I was **lost**.*

lot or lots

A **lot** of something, or **lots** of something, is a large amount of it.
ઘણું બધું
*He drank **lots** of milk.*

loud adjective
louder, loudest

A **loud** noise is a very big sound.
મોટા અવાજવાળું, ધોંઘાટિયું
*The music was very **loud**.*

a b c d e f g h i j k l m n o p q r s t u v w x y z

79

A
B
C
D
E
F
G
H
I
J
K
L
M
N
O
P
Q
R
S
T
U
V
W
X
Y
Z

love *verb*
loves, loving, loved

1 If you **love** someone, you care very much about them.
ચાહવું

2 If you **love** something, you like it very much.
ગમવું, પસંદ પડવું
*We both **love** football.*

lovely *adjective*
lovelier, loveliest

A **lovely** thing or person is very beautiful or very nice.
અત્યંત સુંદર, આનંદદાયક, રોચક, મનોહર
*I thought she looked **lovely**.*

low *adjective*
lower, lowest

1 Something that is **low** is close to the ground.
નીચું
*There is a **low** fence around the house.*

2 A **low** number is a small number.
ઓછું
*The price was very **low**.*

lucky *adjective*
luckier, luckiest

Someone who is **lucky** enjoys good things that people don't expect to happen.
ભાગ્યશાળી, નસીબદાર
*He was **lucky** to win the competition.*

lump *noun*
lumps

A **lump** is a solid piece of something.
લોચો, લોંદો, ગઠ્ઠો, ગાંગડો
*There was a bowl full of **lumps** of sugar.*

lunch *noun*
lunches

Lunch is the meal that you have in the middle of the day.
બપોરનું ખાણું

lying
⇨ Look at **lie**.
*There was a man **lying** on the ground.*

machine *noun*
machines

A **machine** is a piece of equipment that uses electricity or an engine to do something.
યંત્ર
*I left a message on the answering **machine**.*

made
⇨ Look at **make**.
*Mum **made** me a big birthday cake.*

magazine *noun*
magazines

A **magazine** is a thin book with stories and pictures in it.
સામયિક
*I get my favourite **magazine** every Thursday.*

magic *noun*

In stories, **magic** is a special power that allows you to do impossible things.
જાદુ, જંતરમંતર
*By **magic**, the man turned to stone.*

magnet *noun*
magnets

A **magnet** is a piece of metal that attracts iron towards it.
લોહચુંબક

main *adjective*

The **main** thing is the most important one.
મુખ્ય
*That's the **main** reason I want it.*

make *verb*
makes, making, made

1 If you **make** something, you put it together or build it from other things.
રચવું, બનાવવું
*She **makes** all her own clothes.*

2 You can use **make** to show that a person does or says something.
કરવું
*He **made** a phone call.*

3 If you **make** a person do something, they must do it.
ફરજ પાડવી
*Mum **made** me clean the bathroom.*

male *adjective*

A **male** person or animal could become a father.
નર,નરજાતિનું
*All of the pupils were **male**.*

mammal *noun*
mammals

Mammals are animals that feed their babies with milk.
સસ્તન પ્રાણી
*Some **mammals**, like whales, live in the sea.*

man *noun*
men

A **man** is an adult male person.
પુરુષ
*The book is for both **men** and women.*

manage *verb*
manages, managing, managed

If you **manage** something, you control it.
...નું નિયંત્રણ કરવું
*He **managed** the bank for 20 years.*

many *adjective*

If there are **many** people or things, there are a lot of them.
ઘણા, બહુ, સંખ્યાબંધ
*Does he have **many** friends?*

map *noun*
maps

A **map** is a drawing of an area from above. It shows where the roads, rivers and railways are.
નકશો
*You can see the park beside this road on the **map**.*

March *noun*

March is the month after February and before April. It has 31 days.
માર્ચ મહિનો

mark *noun*
marks

1 A **mark** is a small dirty area on a surface.
ધાબું, ડાઘ
*I can't get this **mark** off my shirt.*

2 A **mark** is a shape that you write or draw.
નિશાની કે ચિહ્ન કરવું
*He made a few **marks** with his pen.*

market *noun*
markets

A **market** is a place where people buy and sell things.
બજાર
*There's a **market** in the town centre every Saturday morning.*

marmalade *noun*

Marmalade is jam that is made from oranges.
લીંબુ કે સફરજનમાથી બનતો મુરબ્બો

marry *verb*
marries, marrying, married

When a man and a woman **marry**, they become husband and wife.
પરણવું

mask *noun*
masks

A **mask** is something that you wear over your face to protect or hide it.
મહોરું

a b c d e f g h i j k l m n o p q r s t u v w x y z

81

mat *noun*
mats

A **mat** is a small piece of cloth, wood, or plastic that you put on a table to protect it.
ટેબલ પર રાખવાની નાની સાદડી
*I put my glass on a red **mat**.*

match *noun*
matches

1 A **match** is a small, thin stick that makes a flame when you rub it on a rough surface.
દીવાસળી
*She lit a **match** and held it up to the candle.*

2 A **match** is a game of football, cricket, or some other sport.
હરીફાઈની રમત
*We won all our **matches** last year.*

match *verb*
matches, matching, matched

If one thing **matches** another, they look good together.
બંધબેસતું
*Do these shoes **match** my dress?*

material *noun*
materials

1 **Material** is cloth.
કાપડ
*Her skirt was made from thick black **material**.*

2 A **material** is what something is made of, like rock, glass or plastic.
ચીજ, વસ્તુ
*Wax is a soft **material**.*

maths *noun*

If you learn **maths**, you learn about numbers, shapes, and amounts.
ગણિતશાસ્ત્ર

matter *verb*
matters, mattered

If something **matters** to you, it is important.
મહત્ત્વનું, અગત્યનું
*Never mind, it doesn't **matter**.*

may *verb*

1 If you **may** do something, it is possible that you will do it.
શક્યતા
*I **may** come back next year.*

2 If you **may** do something, you can do it because someone allows you to do it.
પરવાનગી
*Please **may** I leave the room?*

May *noun*

May is the month after April and before June. It has 31 days.
મે મહિનો (અંગ્રેજી કેલેન્ડરનો)

me

You use **me** when you are talking about yourself.
મને, હું, પોતે
*Can you hear **me**?*

meal *noun*
meals

A **meal** is food that you eat at one time. Breakfast, lunch and dinner are **meals**.
ભોજન
*She sat next to me for every **meal**.*

mean *verb*
means, meaning, meant

1 If you ask what something **means**, you want to understand it.
અર્થ કરવો
*What does this word **mean**?*

2 If you **mean** what you are saying, it is not a joke.
નિશ્ચય હોવો
*He says he loves her, and I think he **means** it.*

3 If you **mean** to do something, it is not an accident.
—નો હેતુ હોવો, -નો ઇરાદો હોવો
*I didn't **mean** to drop the cup.*

mean *adjective*
meaner, meanest

Someone who is **mean** is not nice to other people.
હલકું, નીચ, હલકટ
*He was sorry for being **mean** to her.*

measles noun

Measles is an illness that gives you a fever and red spots on your skin.
ઓરી

measure verb
measures, measuring, measured

If you **measure** something, you find its size.
માપ
*First **measure** the length of the table.*

meat noun

Meat is the part of an animal that people cook and eat.
માંસ
*I don't eat **meat** or fish.*

medicine noun

Medicine is something that you swallow to make you better when you are ill.
વૈદકશાસ્ત્ર
*The **medicine** saved his life.*

meet verb
meets, meeting, met

If you **meet** someone, you see them and you talk to them.
મળવું
*I **met** my friends in town today.*

melon noun
melons

A **melon** is a large, soft, sweet fruit with a hard green or yellow skin.
તરબૂચ
*We ate slices of **melon**.*

melt verb
melts, melting, melted

When something **melts**, it changes from a solid to a liquid as it becomes warmer.
ઓગાળવું
__Melt__ the chocolate in a bowl.

memory noun
memories

1 Your **memory** is the part of your mind that remembers things.
યાદશક્તિ, સ્મરણશક્તિ
*He has a very good **memory** for numbers.*

2 A **memory** is something you remember about the past.
સ્મૃતિ
*They discussed their **memories** of their school days.*

men
⇨ Look at **man**.
*He ordered his **men** to stop.*

mend verb
mends, mending, mended

If you **mend** something that is broken, you repair it.
દુરસ્ત કરવું, સુધરવું
*They **mended** the hole in the roof.*

mess noun

If something is a **mess**, it is not neat.
ગંદું, વેરવિખેર
*After the party, the house was a **mess**.*

message noun
messages

A **message** is a piece of information that you send someone.
સંદેશો
*I got emails and **messages** from friends all over the world.*

messy adjective
messier, messiest

A person or thing that is **messy** is not neat.
ગોટાળો કરનારું, અવ્યવસ્થિત, ગંદું
*His writing is rather **messy**.*

met
⇨ Look at **meet**.
*We **met** when we were on holiday.*

a
b
c
d
e
f
g
h
i
j
k
l
m
n
o
p
q
r
s
t
u
v
w
x
y
z

metal *noun*
metals

Metal is a hard material that melts when it gets very hot.
ધાતુ
*Gold, iron and lead are different kinds of **metal**.*

metre *noun*
metres

A **metre** is used for measuring distances or how long things are.
મીટર - લંબાઇનું એકમ- 1 મીટર બરાબર 100 સે.મી.
*The hole in the ground is about one and a half **metres** across.*

mice
➡ Look at **mouse**.
*You can hear the **mice** under the floor.*

midday *noun*
Midday is twelve o'clock in the middle of the day.
બપોર, મધ્યાહ્ન
*At **midday** everyone had lunch.*

middle *noun*
middles

The **middle** of something is the part that is the same distance from each edge or end.
મધ્યસ્થાન કે મધ્યભાગ
*We stood in the **middle** of the room.*

midnight *noun*
Midnight is twelve o'clock at night.
મધરાત
*They went to bed after **midnight**.*

might *verb*
You use **might** when something is possible.
શક્યતા હોવી
*He **might** win the race.*

mile *noun*
miles

A **mile** is used for measuring distance.
માઇલ-અંતરનું એકમ
*They drove 600 **miles** across the desert.*

milk *noun*
Milk is the white liquid that all baby mammals get from their mothers. People also drink **milk** that farmers get from cows.
દૂધ
*They make cheese from goat's and sheep's **milk** too.*

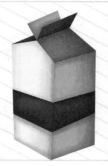

millilitre *noun*
millilitres

A **millilitre** is used for measuring liquid. There are 1,000 **millilitres** in a litre.
એક સહસ્ત્રાંશ લીટર
*I gave him the medicine with a 5 **millilitre** spoon.*

millimetre *noun*
millimetres

A **millimetre** is used for measuring how long things are.
There are 1,000 **millimetres** in a metre.
મિલિમીટર
*The small insect was a few **millimetres** long.*

mind *noun*
minds

Your **mind** is the part of your brain that thinks, understands and remembers.
મગજ
*I can't get that song out of my **mind**.*

mind *verb*
minds, minding, minded

If you **mind** something, it annoys you.
હરકત હોવી, વાંધો હોવો
*It was hard work but she didn't **mind**.*

mine
Mine means belonging to me.
મારું
*That isn't your bag, it's **mine**.*

mine *noun*
mines

A **mine** is a deep hole or tunnel where people go to dig things like gold or diamonds out of rock.
ખાણ

minus

You use **minus** when you take one number away from another number.
ઓછા, બાદ કરતાં

*Three **minus** two is one.*

minute *noun*
minutes

A **minute** is used for measuring time. There are sixty seconds in one **minute**.
મિનિટ

*The food will take 20 **minutes** to cook.*

minute *adjective*

Something that is **minute** is very small.
બહુ ઝીણું, સૂક્ષ્મ
*You only need to use a **minute** amount of glue.*

miss *verb*
misses, missing, missed

1 If you **miss** something that you are trying to hit or catch, you do not manage to hit it or catch it.
ચૂકી જવું
*I jumped, but **missed** the ball.*

2 If you **miss** something, you do not notice it.
સમજવામાં નિષ્ફળ જવું
*What did he say? I **missed** it.*

3 If you **miss** someone who is not with you, you feel sad that they are not there.
ખોટ સાલવી
*The boys **miss** their father.*

Miss

You use **Miss** in front of the name of a girl or a woman who is not married when you are talking to her or talking about her.
અપરિણીત સ્ત્રીના નામની પૂર્વે વપરાતો શબ્દ

*Do you know **Miss** Smith?*

mistake *noun*
mistakes

A **mistake** is something that is not correct.
ભૂલ કરવી
*I made three **mistakes** in my letter.*

mix *verb*
mixes, mixing, mixed

If you **mix** things, you put different things together to make something new.
ભેળવવું, મિશ્રણ કરવું
Mix the sugar with the butter.

mixture *noun*
mixtures

A **mixture** is what you make when you mix different things together.
મિશ્રણ

*The drink is a **mixture** of orange and apple juice.*

mobile phone *noun*
mobile phones

A **mobile phone** is a small phone that you can take everywhere with you.
મોબાઇલ ફોન

model *noun*
models

1 A **model** is a small copy of something.
નમૂનો, પ્રતિકૃતિ
*I made the **model** house with paper and glue.*

2 A **model** is a person whose job is to wear and show new clothes.
કપડાં કેવાં દેખાય છે તે બતાવનાર વ્યક્તિ
*The **model** in the picture was very tall.*

mole *noun*
moles

1 A **mole** is a natural dark spot on your skin.
શરીર પરનો તલ, મસો
*She has a **mole** on the side of her nose.*

2 A **mole** is a small animal with black fur that lives under the ground.
છછુંદર, ચેન

A B C D E F G H I J K L **M** N O P Q R S T U V W X Y Z

moment noun
moments

A **moment** is a very short period of time.
પળ
He stopped for a moment.

Monday noun
Mondays

Monday is the day after Sunday and before Tuesday.
સોમવાર
I went back to school on Monday.

money noun

Money is what you use to buy things.
પૈસા
Cars cost a lot of money.

monkey noun
monkeys

A **monkey** is an animal that has a long tail and can climb trees.
વાંદરો

monster noun
monsters

In stories, a **monster** is a big, ugly creature that frightens people.
ડરામણું મહાકાય પ્રાણી
The film is about a monster in the wardrobe.

month noun
months

A **month** is one part of a year. There are twelve **months** in one year.
મહિનો
We are going on holiday next month.

moon noun
moons

The **moon** shines in the sky at night and moves around the earth every month.
ચંદ્ર
The first man on the moon was Neil Armstrong.

more

You use **more** to talk about a greater amount of something.
વધુ, વધારે, અધિક
He has more chips than me.

morning noun
mornings

The **morning** is the early part of the day, before lunch.
સવાર
What do you want to do tomorrow morning?

most

1   **Most** of a group of things or people means nearly all of them.
મોટા ભાગનું
Most of the houses here are very old.

2   The **most** means the largest amount.
સૌથી વધુ (જથામાં, માત્રામાં કે)
Who has the most money?

moth noun
moths

A **moth** is an insect like a butterfly that usually flies at night.
મોથ - એક નાનું જીવડું

mother noun
mothers

A **mother** is a woman who has a child.
મા

motorbike noun
motorbikes

A **motorbike** is a large bike with an engine.
ઍન્જિનવાળી બાઇસિકલ

motorway *noun*
motorways

A **motorway** is a wide road for travelling long distances fast.
રાજમાર્ગ

mountain *noun*
mountains

A **mountain** is a very high area of land with steep sides.
પહાડ

*Ben Nevis is the highest **mountain** in Scotland.*

mouse *noun*
mice

1 A **mouse** is a small animal with a long tail.
ઉંદર

2 You use a **mouse** to move things on a computer screen.
કમ્પ્યૂટરનું માઉસ

mouth *noun*
mouths

Your **mouth** is the part of your face that you use for eating or talking.
મોઢું

*When you cough, please cover your **mouth**.*

move *verb*
moves, moving, moved

1 When you **move** something, you put it in a different place.
ખસવું, હલાવવું, ખસેડવું
*The man asked her to **move** her car.*

2 If you **move**, you go to live in a different place.
સ્થાન પરિવર્તન કરવું
*She's **moving** to London next month.*

Mr

You use **Mr** before a man's name when you are talking to him or talking about him.
શ્રી

*Our history teacher's name is **Mr** Jones.*

Mrs

You use **Mrs** before a married woman's name when you are talking to her or talking about her.
શ્રીમતી

*How are you, **Mrs** Smith?*

Ms

You use **Ms** before a woman's name when you are talking to her or talking about her.
સુશ્રી

*The message is for **Ms** Clark.*

much

You use **much** to talk about a large amount of something.
ધણું, બહુ, પુષ્કળ
*I ate too **much** food.*

mud *noun*

Mud is a mixture of earth and water.
કાદવ
*There was thick **mud** on my football boots.*

muddy *adjective*
muddier, muddiest

If something is **muddy**, it is covered with mud.
કાદવવાળું
*My boots are all **muddy**!*

mug *noun*
mugs

A **mug** is a deep cup with straight sides.
સીધા ઘાટનો પ્યાલો
*He poured tea into the **mugs**.*

a
b
c
d
e
f
g
h
i
j
k
l
m
n
o
p
q
r
s
t
u
v
w
x
y
z

A B C D E F G H I J K L M N O P Q R S T U V W X Y Z

multiplication *noun*
Multiplication is when you multiply one number by another.
ગુણવું તે, ગુણાકાર

multiply *verb*
multiplies, multiplying, multiplied
If you **multiply** a number, you add it to itself a number of times.
ગુણાકાર કરવો
*You get 24 if you **multiply** three by eight.*

mum *or* mummy *noun*
mums or **mummies**
Mum or **mummy** is a name for your mother.
મા

muscle *noun*
muscles
Your **muscles** are the parts inside your body that help you move.
સ્નાયુ
*Sport helps to keep your **muscles** strong.*

museum *noun*
museums
A **museum** is a building where you can look at interesting, old, and valuable things.
સંગ્રહાલય
*Hundreds of people came to the **museum** to see the dinosaur bones.*

mushroom *noun*
mushrooms
A **mushroom** is a plant with a short stem and a round top that you can eat.
બિલાડીનો ટોપ
*There are many types of wild **mushroom**, and some of them are poisonous.*

music *noun*
Music is the sound that you make when you sing or play instruments.
સંગીત
*What's your favourite **music**?*

musical instrument *noun*
musical instruments
A **musical instrument** is an instrument that you use to play music, like a piano or a guitar.
સંગીતનું વાઘ કે વાજું

must *verb*
You use **must** to show that you think something is very important.
આવશ્યકતા કે ભાર દર્શાવનારૂં સહાયકારક ક્રિયાપદ
*You **must** tell the police all the facts.*

mustn't
Mustn't is short for **must not**.
ન કરવું જોઈએ
*I **mustn't** forget to take my key with me.*

my
You use **my** to show that something belongs to you.
મારું
*I went to sleep in **my** room.*

myself
You use **myself** when the you are talking about yourself.
મારી જાતે, હું પોતે
*I hurt **myself** when I fell down.*

mystery *noun*
mysteries
A **mystery** is something that you do not understand or know about.
કોયડો
*Why she's crying is a **mystery**.*

myth *noun*
myths
A **myth** is a very old story about magic, and strange people and creatures.
પ્રાચીન દંતકથા, પુરાણકથા

Nn

nail *noun*
nails

1 A **nail** is a thin piece of metal. It is flat at one end and it has a point at the other end.
ખીલો, ચૂંક, ખીલી
*A picture hung on a **nail** in the wall.*

2 Your **nails** are the thin hard parts that grow at the ends of your fingers and toes.
નખ
*Try to keep your **nails** short.*

name *noun*
names

A person's **name** is the word or words that you use to talk to them, or to talk about them.
નામ
*Is your **name** Peter?*

narrow *adjective*
narrower, narrowest

Something that is **narrow** is a small distance from one side to the other.
સાંકડું, લંબાઈના પ્રમાણમાં ઓછું
*We walked through the town's **narrow** streets.*

nasty *adjective*
nastier, nastiest

Something that is **nasty** is horrible.
સૂગ ચડે એવું મેલું, ગંદું
*That's a **nasty** thing to say!*

natural *adjective*

Natural things come from nature.
કુદરતી, સ્વાભાવિક,
*The **natural** home of these animals is under the ground.*

nature *noun*

Nature is all the animals, plants, and other things in the world that people did not make or change.
પ્રકૃતિ
*We watched **nature** all around us from our camp in the forest.*

naughty *adjective*
naughtier, naughtiest

A **naughty** child does things which are bad.
દુર્વર્તની, તોફાની, કહ્યું ન કરનારું,
*She was so **naughty**, her mother sent her to bed early.*

near *adjective*
nearer, nearest

If something is **near** a place, thing, or person, it is not far away from them.
નજીક
*We are very **near** my house.*

nearly

Nearly means almost.
લગભગ, ધણુંખરું
*It's **nearly** five o'clock.*

neat *adjective*
neater, neatest

A **neat** place or person is clean and tidy.
સ્વચ્છ
*She made sure that her room was **neat** before she left.*

neck *noun*
necks

Your **neck** is the part of your body between your head and the rest of your body.
ગરદન, ડોક
*He wore a gold chain around his **neck**.*

necklace *noun*
necklaces

A **necklace** is a chain of beads or jewels that you wear around your neck.
હાર (ગળામાં પહેરવાનો)
*She's wearing a beautiful **necklace**.*

need *verb*
needs, needing, needed

If you **need** something, you believe that you must have it or do it.
જરૂરી હોવું
*I **need** some more money.*

needle *noun*
needles

A **needle** is a small, thin metal tool with a sharp point that you use for sewing.
સોય, સોયો
*If you get me a **needle** and thread, I'll sew the button on.*

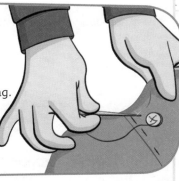

needn't
Needn't is short for **need not**.
ન કરો
*You **needn't** come with us if you don't want to.*

neighbour *noun*
neighbours

Your **neighbours** are the people who live around you.
પડોસી
*I met our **neighbour** when I went to the shops.*

nephew *noun*
nephews

Someone's **nephew** is the son of their sister or brother.
ભત્રીજો
*I have a **nephew** who is still a baby.*

nervous *adjective*

If you are **nervous** about something, it worries you and you are rather afraid.
નબળા મનનું, સહેજમાં
*I tried not to show that I was **nervous**.*

nest *noun*
nests

A **nest** is the place where a bird keeps its eggs or its babies.
પક્ષીનો માળો
*There were six small eggs in the bird's **nest**.*

net *noun*
nets

A **net** is made from pieces of string or rope tied together with holes between them. It is for catching things like fish, or the ball in some sports.
જાળી, (દોરા, દોરી, તાર વગેરેની)
*The idea is to throw the ball into the top of the **net**.*

never
Never means at no time in the past, present or future.
કદી નહિ, ક્યારેય નહિ
***Never** look straight at the sun.*

new *adjective*
newer, newest

1 Something that is **new** was not there before.
નવું
*They discovered a **new** medicine for his illness.*

2 If something is **new**, nobody has used it before.
હવે પહેલવહેલું બનેલું
*I am wearing my **new** shoes.*

3 A **new** thing or person is a different one from the one you had before.
બદલાયેલું
*We have a **new** history teacher.*

news *noun*
News is information that you did not know before.
સમાચાર
*We waited and waited for **news** of him.*

newspaper *noun*
newspapers

A **newspaper** is a number of large sheets of paper with news and other information printed on them.
અખબાર, વર્તમાનપત્ર
*They read about it in the **newspaper**.*

next *adjective*

The **next** thing is the one that comes immediately after this one or after the last one.
તરત પછીનું
*I got up early the **next** morning.*

nice *adjective*
nicer, nicest

If something is **nice**, you like it.
સરસ, સુંદર
*They live in a really **nice** house.*

niece *noun*
nieces

Someone's **niece** is the daughter of their sister or brother.
ભત્રીજી
*He bought a present for his **niece**.*

night *noun*
nights

The **night** is the time when it is dark outside, and most people sleep.
રાત
*It's eleven o'clock at **night** in Beijing.*

nightdress *noun*
nightdresses

A **nightdress** is a loose dress that a woman or girl can wear to sleep in.
રાત્રે પહેરવાનો ઢીલો પોશાક

nightmare *noun*
nightmares

A **nightmare** is a dream that frightens or worries you.
ભીષણ સ્વપ્ન
*She had a **nightmare** last night.*

nine

Nine is the number .
નવ

no

You use **no** to say that something is not true or to refuse something.
ના, નહિ
*"Would you like a drink?"—"**No** thank you."*

nobody *noun*

Nobody means not one person.
કોઈ નહીં
*For a long time, **nobody** spoke.*

nod *verb*
nods, nodding, nodded

When you **nod**, you move your head up and down, usually to show that you agree.
હકારમાં માથું હલાવવું
*She **nodded** and smiled.*

noise *noun*
noises

A **noise** is a loud sound.
કોલાહલ, બુમરાણ, શોરબકોર
*Suddenly there was a **noise** like thunder.*

noisy *adjective*
noisier, noisiest

A **noisy** person or thing makes a lot of loud noise.
ઘોંઘાટ કરનારૂં, ધમાલિયું
*It was a very **noisy** party.*

none

None means not one or not any.
કોઈ નહીં, એક પણ નહિ
***None** of us knew her.*

nonsense *noun*

If something is **nonsense**, it is not true or it is silly.
બકવાસ
*My father said the story was **nonsense**.*

noon *noun*

Noon is twelve o'clock in the middle of the day.
બપોર
*The lesson started at **noon**.*

a
b
c
d
e
f
g
h
i
j
k
l
m
n
o
p
q
r
s
t
u
v
w
x
y
z

A
B
C
D
E
F
G
H
I
J
K
L
M
N
O
P
Q
R
S
T
U
V
W
X
Y
Z

north *noun*

The **north** is the direction to your left when you are looking towards the place where the sun rises.
ઉત્તર દિશા

nose *noun*
noses

Your **nose** is the part of your face above your mouth that you use for breathing and for noticing smells.
નાક
*She sneezed and blew her **nose**.*

nostril *noun*
nostrils

Your **nostrils** are the two holes at the end of your nose.
નસકોરું
*Keeping your mouth closed, breathe in through your **nostrils**.*

note *noun*
notes

1 A **note** is a short letter or message.
   નોંધ
   *He wrote her a **note** and left it on the table.*

2 A **note** is one musical sound.
   સંગીતનો સ્વર કે સૂર
   *She played some **notes** on her recorder.*

nothing

Nothing means not anything.
કશું નહિ, કંઈ નહિ, જરાય નહિ
*There was **nothing** to do.*

notice *verb*
notices, noticing, noticed

If you **notice** something, you suddenly see or hear it.
નજર કરવી
*Did you **notice** him leave the room?*

notice *noun*
notices

A **notice** is a sign that gives information or instructions.
નોટીસ,સૂચના, ખબર
*The **notice** said "Please close the door."*

noun *noun*
nouns

A **noun** is a word that is used for talking about a person or thing. Examples of **nouns** are "child", "table", "sun", and "strength".
સંજ્ઞા

November *noun*

November is the month after October and before December. It has 30 days.
ખ્રિસ્તી વર્ષનો અગિયારમો મહિનો

now

You use **now** to talk about the present time.
હાલ, હમણાં, થોડા વખત પર
*I must go **now**.*

nowhere

Nowhere means not anywhere.
ક્યાંય નહિ
*There's **nowhere** quiet for me to do my homework.*

number *noun*
numbers

A **number** is a word that you use to count.
નંબર, સંખ્યા
*What **number** is your house?*

nurse *noun*
nurses

A **nurse** is a person whose job is to care for people who are ill.
માંદાની સેવા કરનાર વ્યક્તિ
*She thanked the **nurses** at the hospital.*

nut *noun*
nuts

A **nut** is a dry fruit with a hard shell.
કોટલાથી ઢંકાયેલું ગરવાળું ફળ
Nuts and seeds are very good for you.

Oo

oak *noun*
oaks
An **oak** tree is a big, tall tree with a wide trunk. Its wood is good for making furniture.
ઓકનું ઝાડ

oar *noun*
oars
An **oar** is a long piece of wood with a wide, flat end, used for moving a boat through the water.
હલેસું

obey *verb*
obeys, obeying, obeyed
If you **obey** a person or an order, you do what you are told to do.
આજ્ઞા પાળવી

ocean *noun*
oceans
An **ocean** is a big sea.
મહાસાગર
We crossed the Atlantic Ocean.

o'clock *noun*
You say **o'clock** when saying what time it is.
વાગે (ઘડીયાળનો સમય)
*It is eight **o'clock** in the morning.*

octagon *noun*
octagons
An **octagon** is a shape with eight straight sides.
અષ્ટકોણ, અષ્ટભુજ

October *noun*
October is the month after September and before November. It has 31 days.
ઑકટોબર

octopus *noun*
octopuses
An **octopus** is a soft ocean animal with eight long arms.
ઑક્ટોપસ-આઠ પગોવાળું એક જળચર પ્રાણી

odd *adjective*
odder, oddest
1 If something is **odd**, it is strange or unusual.
વિચિત્ર
*There was an **odd** smell in the kitchen.*

2 You say that two things are **odd** when they do not belong to the same set or pair.
અસાધારણ
*I'm wearing **odd** socks.*

3 **Odd** numbers, such as 3 and 17, are numbers that cannot be divided by the number two.
વિષમ અથવા એકી સંખ્યાનું

off
1 If you take something **off** another thing, it is no longer on it.
આઘે, દૂર, અંતર પર
*He took his feet **off** the desk.*

2 When something that uses electricity is **off**, it is not using electricity.
બંધ પડેલું
*The light was **off**.*

offer *verb*
offers, offering, offered
If you **offer** something to someone, you ask them if they would like to have it.
દરખાસ્ત કરવી
*He **offered** his seat to the young woman.*

office *noun*
offices

An **office** is a room where people work at desks.
કાર્યાલય

often

Something that happens **often** happens many times or a lot of the time.
અવારનવાર, ઘણી વાર

oil *noun*

Oil is a thick liquid.
તેલ
*We need some cooking **oil**.*

old *adjective*
older, oldest

1 An **old** person is someone who has lived for a long time.
વયોવૃદ્ધ
*An **old** lady sat next to me.*

2 An **old** thing is something that somebody made a long time ago.
જૂના વખતનું
*We have a very **old** car.*

on

1 If someone or something is **on** a surface, it is resting there.
ઉપર
*There was a large box **on** the table.*

2 When something that uses electricity is **on**, it is using electricity.
ચાલુ
*The television is **on**.*

once

If something happens **once**, it happens one time only.
એકવખત
*I met her **once**, at a party.*

one *noun*

One is the number **1**.
એકની સંખ્યા અથવા આંકડો

onion *noun*
onions

An **onion** is a small, round vegetable with a brown skin like paper and a very strong taste.
ડુંગળી

only

1 If you talk about the **only** thing or person, you mean that there are no others.
એકજ
*It was the **only** shop in the town.*

2 You use **only** when you are saying how small or short something is.
ફકત, માત્ર
*Their house is **only** a few miles from here.*

3 If you are an **only** child, you have no brothers or sisters.
એકલું જ

open *verb*
opens, opening, opened

1 When you **open** something, or when it **opens**, you move it so that it is no longer closed.
ખુલ્લું, ઉઘાડું
*She **opened** the door.*

2 When a shop or office **opens**, people are able to go in.
બધાંને માટે ખુલ્લું કે છૂટવાળું
*The banks will **open** again on Monday morning.*

opposite

1 If one thing is **opposite** another, it is across from it.
સામે, સન્મુખ
*Jennie sat **opposite** Sam at breakfast.*

2 If things are **opposite**, they are as different as they can be.
ઊલટું, વિરોધી, વિપરીત
*We watched the cars driving in the **opposite** direction.*

orange *noun*

1 An **orange** is a round fruit with a thick skin and lots of juice.
સંતરું

2 **Orange** is a colour between red and yellow.
નારંગી રંગ
*Tigers are **orange** with black stripes.*

orchestra *noun*
orchestras

An **orchestra** is a large group of people who play music together.
વાદકવૃંદ
*The **orchestra** began to play.*

A B C D E F G H I J K L M N O P Q R S T U V W X Y Z

order *verb*
orders, ordering, ordered
If you **order** someone to do something, you tell them to do it.
હુકમ કરવો, આદેશ આપવો
*She **ordered** him to leave.*

ordinary *adjective*
Ordinary means not special or different in any way.
સાધારણ
*It was just an **ordinary** day.*

other *adjective*
others
Other people or things are different people or things.
બીજું, અન્ય
*All the **other** children had gone home.*

our
You use **our** to show that something belongs to you and one or more other people.
અમારું, આપણું
__Our__ house is near the school.

ours
You use **ours** when you are talking about something that belongs to you and one or more other people.
આપણું, અમારું
*That car is **ours**.*

out
1 If you go **out** of a place, you leave it.
બહાર
*She ran **out** of the house.*

2 If you are **out**, you are not at home.
ઘરની બહાર
*I called you yesterday, but you were **out**.*

3 If a light is **out**, it is no longer shining.
હોલવાયેલું, બળતું
*All the lights were **out** in the house.*

outside
1 The **outside** of something is the part that covers the rest of it.
બહારની બાજુ
*They are painting the **outside** of the building.*

2 If you are **outside**, you are not in a building.
બહાર
*Let's play **outside**.*

oval *adjective*
Oval things have a shape like an egg.
લંબગોળ
*She has an **oval** table.*

oven *noun*
ovens
An **oven** is the part of a cooker like a large metal box with a door.
રાંધવા-પકાવવાની નાની ભઠ્ઠી, ઓવન

over
1 If one thing is **over** another thing, the first thing is above or higher than the second thing.
ઉપર, પર
*There was a lamp **over** the table.*

2 If something is **over**, it has finished.
પૂરું, ખલાસ, સમાપ્ત, ખતમ
*The class is **over**.*

owe *verb*
owes, owing, owed
If you **owe** money to someone, you have to pay money to them.
-ના ઋણી હોવું
*He **owes** him $50.*

owl *noun*
owls
An **owl** is a bird with large eyes that hunts at night.
ઘુવડ

own
You use **own** to say that something belongs to you.
પોતાનું, અંગત
*Jennifer wanted her **own** room.*

ox *noun*
oxen
An **ox** is a kind of bull that is used for carrying or pulling things.
બળદ

pack verb
packs, packing, packed

When you **pack** a bag, you put clothes and other things into it, because you are going away.
કપડાં ઇ. થેલીમાં ભરવું,

paddle noun
paddles

A **paddle** is a short oar. You use it to move a small boat through water.
નાનું હલેસું, હોડીનો ચાટવો

paddle verb
paddles, paddling, paddled

1 If someone **paddles** a boat, they move it using a paddle.
હલેસું મારવું

2 If you **paddle**, you walk in shallow water.
છીછરા પાણીમાં ઉઘાડે પગે ચાલવું

page noun
pages

A **page** is one side of a piece of paper in a book, a magazine, or a newspaper.
પાનું

Turn to page 4.

paid
➡ Look at **pay**.
Daddy paid for the sweets.

pain noun
pains

Pain is the feeling that you have in a part of your body, because of illness or an accident.
પીડા

I felt a sudden sharp pain in my ankle.

painful adjective

If a part of your body is **painful**, it hurts.
પીડાકારક

His right knee is very painful.

paint noun
paints

Paint is a liquid used to decorate buildings, or to make a picture.
રંગ

Can I use some of your red paint?

paint verb
paints, painting, painted

1 If you **paint** something on a piece of paper or cloth, you make a picture of it using paint.
રંગથી ચિત્ર ચીતરવું
He likes painting flowers.

2 If you **paint** a wall or a door, you cover it with paint.
રંગનો હાથ દેવો

painting noun
paintings

A **painting** is a picture made with paint.
રંગીન ચિત્ર

He's doing a painting of a bowl of fruit.

pair noun
pairs

A **pair** of things is two things of the same size and shape that are used together.
જોડી કે જોડ્

She wore a pair of plain black shoes.

palace noun
palaces

A **palace** is a very large house where important people live.
રાજમહેલ

pale adjective
paler, palest

A **pale** colour is not strong or bright.
ફીકું

She's wearing a pale blue dress.

palm *noun*
palms

1 A **palm** or a **palm tree** is a tree that grows in hot countries. It has long leaves at the top, and no branches.
તાડનું ઝાડ

2 The **palm** of your hand is the inside part of your hand, between your fingers and your wrist.
હથેળી,હથેલી

panda *noun*
pandas

A **panda** is a large animal with black and white fur.
પાન્ડા- રીંછ જેવું ચીનનું કદાવર પ્રાણી

pantomime *noun*
pantomimes

A **pantomime** is a play that has a funny story with music and songs.
બાળકો માટેનું મૂક રમૂજી સંગીતમય નાટક

paper *noun*
papers

1 **Paper** is a material that you write on or wrap things with.
કાગળ
*He wrote his name down on a piece of **paper**.*

2 A **paper** is a newspaper.
છાપું, સમાચાર પત્ર

parcel *noun*
parcels

A **parcel** is something that is wrapped in paper.
પડીકું...ટપાલ દ્વારા મોકલવામાં આવતું પડીકું, પાર્સલ

parent *noun*
parents

Your **parents** are your mother and father.
માતા કે પિતા

park *noun*
parks

A **park** is a place with grass and trees. People go to **parks** to take exercise or play games.
બાગ, બગીચો

park *verb*
parks, parking, parked

When someone **parks** a car, they leave it somewhere.
કોઈ જગ્યાએ વાહન ઊભું રાખવું
*They **parked** in the street outside the house.*

parrot *noun*
parrots

A **parrot** is a bird with a curved beak and bright feathers.
પોપટ

Parrots' feet have two toes at the front and two at the back.

part *noun*
parts

Part of something is a piece of it.
અંશ

party *noun*
parties

A **party** is a time when people meet to have fun.
મિજબાની, મિજલસ
She's having a birthday party.

pass *verb*
passes, passing, passed

1 When you **pass** someone, you go by them.
પસાર થવું
*We **passed** them on our way here.*

2 If you **pass** something to someone, you give it to them.
પસાર કરવું
*He **passed** a note to his friend.*

3 If you **pass** a test, you do well.
સફળ થવું

passenger *noun*
passengers

A **passenger** is a person who is travelling in a vehicle, but who is not driving.
મુસાફર

A
B
C
D
E
F
G
H
I
J
K
L
M
N
O
P
Q
R
S
T
U
V
W
X
Y
Z

past *noun*

The **past** is the period of time before now.
ભૂતકાળ
*In the **past**, there weren't any computers.*

past

1 Something that is **past** a place is on the other side of it.
-ની આગળ, -ની પેલે પાર
*It's just **past** the school there.*

2 You use **past** when you are telling the time.
વીતી ગયેલું
*It was ten **past** eleven.*

pasta *noun*

Pasta is a mixture of flour, eggs, and water.
લોટ, ઇંડું અને પાણીના મિશ્રણથી બનાવાતી વાનગી
Pasta comes in lots of shapes, even letters of the alphabet.

paste *verb*
pastes, pasting, pasted

1 If you **paste** something on to a surface, you stick it with glue.
ચોટાડવું

2 If you **paste** words or pictures on a computer, you copy them from one place and put them somewhere new.
કમ્પ્યૂટરમાં શબ્દ કે પાઠ ચોક્કસ જગાએ ખસેડવો
*You can **paste** by holding down the Ctrl key and pressing V.*

pastry *noun*

Pastry is a mixture of flour, butter, and water. People make it flat and thin so that they can use it to make pies.
લોટ, પાણી અને ચરબીથી બનાવાયેલો ખોરાક, તેમાંથી બનાવેલી વાનગી

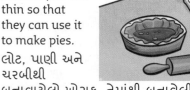

path *noun*
paths

A **path** is a strip of ground that people walk along.
પગદંડી
*We followed the **path** along the cliff.*

patient *adjective*

If you are **patient**, you don't get angry quickly.
ધીરજવાળું, સહનશીલ

patient *noun*
patients

A **patient** is someone that a nurse or a doctor is looking after.
રોગી, દરદી

pattern *noun*
patterns

A **pattern** is a group of repeated shapes.
નકશી, ભાત
*The carpet had a **pattern** of light and dark stripes.*

paw *noun*
paws

The **paws** of an animal such as a cat, dog, or bear are its feet.
નહોરવાળાં પ્રાણીનો પંજો
*The kitten was black with white **paws**.*

pay *verb*
pays, paying, paid

If you **pay** for something, you give someone an amount of money for it.
પૈસા ચૂકવવા ભરવા કે આપવા
*Did you **pay** for those sweets?*

peach *noun*
peaches

A **peach** is a round fruit with a soft red and orange skin.
આલૂ

peanut *noun*
peanuts

Peanuts are small nuts that you can eat.
મગફળી

pear *noun*
pears

A **pear** is a fruit which is narrow at the top and wide and round at the bottom.
નાસપતી

peas *noun*

Peas are small, round, green vegetables.
વટાણા

pebble *noun*
pebbles

A **pebble** is a small, smooth stone.
કાંકરી

pedal *noun*
pedals

The **pedals** on a bicycle are the two parts that you push with your feet to make the bicycle move.
સાઇકલ ચલાવવાની પાવડી

peel *noun*

The **peel** of a fruit is its skin.
છાલ

peg *noun*
pegs

A **peg** is a small piece of metal or wood on a wall that you hang things on.
દીવાલ અથવા બારણાં પર વસ્તુઓ ભેરવવાનું નાનું કડું કે હૂક

pen *noun*
pens

A **pen** is a long thin tool that you use for writing with ink.
કલમ

pencil *noun*
pencils

A **pencil** is a thin piece of wood with a black material through the middle that you use to write or draw with.
સીસાપેન, પેન્સિલ

penguin *noun*
penguins

A **penguin** is a black and white bird that lives in very cold places. **Penguins** can swim but they cannot fly.
પેન્ગવિન, ઉડી ન શકનારું, દક્ષિણ ધ્રુવનું પંખી

pentagon *noun*
pentagons

A **pentagon** is a shape with five straight sides.
પંચકોણ, પંચભુજ

people *noun*

People are men, women, and children.
લોકો
*Lots of **people** came to the party.*

pepper *noun*
peppers

1 **Pepper** is a powder with a hot taste that you put on food.
મરીનું ચૂર્ણ
2 A **pepper** is a green, red, or yellow vegetable with seeds inside it.
શાકભાજીમાં વપરાતું લાલ, લીલું કે પીળું મરચું

period *noun*
periods

A **period** is a length of time.
સમયગાળો

person *noun*
people

A **person** is a man, a woman, or a child.
વ્યક્તિ

pest *noun*
pests

Pests are insects or small animals that damage crops or food.
ઉપદ્રવકારી જંતુ કે પ્રાણી

pet *noun*
pets

A **pet** is a tame animal that you keep in your home.
પાલતુ પ્રાણી

a b c d e f g h i j k l m n o p q r s t u v w x y z

A
B
C
D
E
F
G
H
I
J
K
L
M
N
O
P
Q
R
S
T
U
V
W
X
Y
Z

petal *noun*
petals

The **petals** of a flower are the thin parts on the outside that are a bright colour.
પાંખડી

phone *noun*
phones

A **phone** is a piece of equipment that you use to talk to someone in another place.
ટેલિફોન

*Two minutes later the **phone** rang.*

photograph *noun*
photographs

A **photograph** is a picture that you take with a camera.
ફોટો, છબી, તસવીર

*She took lots of **photographs** of her friends.*

piano *noun*
pianos

A **piano** is a large instrument for playing music. You play it by pressing the black and white keys.
પિયાનો-સંગીત વાદ્ય

pick *verb*
picks, picking, picked

1 If you **pick** someone, you choose them.
   પસંદ કરવું

2 When you **pick** flowers, fruit, or leaves, you take them from a plant or tree.
   ચૂંટવું

   *I've **picked** some flowers from the garden.*

picnic *noun*
picnics

When people have a **picnic**, they eat a meal outside, usually in a park or a forest, or at the beach.
વનભોજન સાથેની સહેલ

*We're going on a **picnic** tomorrow.*

picture *noun*
pictures

A **picture** is a drawing or painting.
ચિત્ર

pie *noun*
pies

A **pie** is a dish of fruit, meat, or vegetables that is covered with pastry and baked.
પેસ્ટ્રીમાં શેકવામાં આવેલાં માંસ, સફરજન, શાકભાજી અથવા તો ફળમાંથી બનાવેલી વાનગી

*We each had a slice of apple **pie**.*

piece *noun*
pieces

A **piece** of something is a part of it.
ટુકડો

*You must only take one **piece** of cake.*

pig *noun*
pigs

A **pig** is a farm animal with a fat body and short legs.
ભૂંડ

pigeon *noun*
pigeons

A **pigeon** is a large grey bird.
કબૂતર

pile *noun*
piles

A **pile** of things is several of them lying on top of each other.
ઢગલો

*We searched through the **pile** of boxes.*

pill *noun*
pills

Pills are small solid round pieces of medicine that you swallow.
ગોળી

pillow *noun*
pillows

A **pillow** is something soft that you rest your head on when you are in bed.
ઓશીકું

pilot *noun*
pilots

A **pilot** is a person who controls an aircraft.
વિમાનચાલક

pin *noun*
pins

A **pin** is a very small thin piece of metal with a point at one end.
ટાંકણી

pineapple *noun*
pineapples

A **pineapple** is a large sweet yellow fruit with a lot of juice. Its skin is brown, thick, and very rough.
અનેનાસ કે અનાનસ

pipe *noun*
pipes

A **pipe** is a long tube that water or gas can flow through.
નળી

*They are going to take out the old water **pipes**.*

pirate *noun*
pirates

Pirates are people who attack ships and steal things from them.
ચાંચિયા

*They have to find the **pirates** and the hidden gold.*

pizza *noun*
pizzas

A **pizza** is a flat, round piece of bread. **Pizzas** are covered with cheese and tomatoes.
પિઝ્ઝા- એક ઇટાલિયન વાનગી

*Bake the **pizza** in a hot oven.*

place *noun*
places

1 A **place** is a building, area, town, or country.
રહેઠાણ, મકાન,શહેર, વિસ્તાર
*This is the **place** where I was born.*

2 A **place** is also where something belongs.
જગ્યા, સ્થળ, સ્થાન
*He put the picture back in its **place** on the shelf.*

plain *adjective*
plainer, plainest

Something that is **plain** is ordinary and not special.
સરળ

plan *noun*
plans

A **plan** is a way of doing something that you work out before you do it.
યોજના

*I've got a **plan** for getting out of here.*

plane *noun*
planes

A **plane** is a large vehicle with wings and engines that flies through the air.
વિમાન

planet *noun*
planets

You find **planets** in space. They move around stars. The Earth is a **planet**.
ઉપગ્રહ

plant *noun*
plants

A **plant** is a living thing that grows in the earth. **Plants** have a stem, leaves, and roots.
છોડ

plaster *noun*
plasters

1 A **plaster** is a strip of material with a soft part in the middle. You can cover a cut on your body with a **plaster**.
મલમપટ્ટી

2 **Plaster** is a paste which people put on walls and ceilings so that they are smooth.
પ્લાસ્ટર
There were huge cracks in the plaster.

plastic *noun*

Plastic is a material that is light but strong. It is made in factories.
પ્લાસ્ટિક
He put his sweets in a plastic bag.

plate *noun*
plates

A **plate** is a flat dish that is used for holding food.
થાળી, તાસક
She pushed her plate away.

platform *noun*
platforms

A **platform** in a station is the place where you wait for a train.
સ્ટેશન પર ગાડીમાંથી ઉતરવા ચડવા માટે

play *verb*
plays, playing, played

1 When you **play**, you spend time using toys and taking part in games.
રમવું
She was playing with her dolls.

2 If you **play** an instrument, you make music with it.
વગાડવું

playground *noun*
playgrounds

A **playground** is a special area where children can play.
રમતનું મેદાન

please

You say **please** when you are asking someone to do something.
મહેરબાની કરીને
Can you help us, please?

plenty *noun*

If there is **plenty** of something, there is a lot of it.
વિપુલ, પૂરતું
Don't worry. There's still plenty of time.

plough *noun*
ploughs

A **plough** is a large tool that is used on a farm. Farmers pull it across a field to make the earth loose, so that they can plant seeds.
હળ

plus

You say **plus** to show that you are adding one number to another.
ના ઉમેરા સાથે
Two plus two is four.

pocket *noun*
pockets

A **pocket** is a small bag that is part of your clothes.
ખિસ્સું
He put the key in his pocket.

poem *noun*
poems

A **poem** is a piece of writing. When people write a **poem**, they choose the words in a very careful way, so that they sound beautiful.
કવિતા

point *noun*
points

1   The **point** of something is its thin, sharp end. Needles and knives have **points**.
અણીદાર છેડો

2   A **point** is a mark that you win in a game or a sport.
ગુણ, માર્ક

point *verb*
points, pointing, pointed

If you **point** at something, you stick out your finger to show where it is.
નિર્દેશ કરવો, બતાવવું
*I **pointed** at the boy sitting near me.*

poisonous *adjective*

Something that is **poisonous** will kill you or hurt you if you swallow or touch it.
ઝેરી

polar bear *noun*
polar bears

A **polar bear** is a large white bear which lives in the area around the North Pole.
ધ્રુવીય રીંછ

police

The **police** are the people who make sure that people obey the law.
પોલીસ

polite *adjective*

Someone who is **polite** behaves well.
વિનમ્ર

pond *noun*
ponds

A **pond** is a small area of water.
તળાવ
*We can feed the ducks on the **pond**.*

pony *noun*
ponies

A **pony** is a small horse.
ટટ્ટુ

poor *adjective*
poorer, poorest

Someone who is **poor** doesn't have much money and doesn't own many things.
ગરીબ

possible *adjective*

If something is **possible** it can happen.
થઇ શકે તેવું

post *verb*
posts, posting, posted

If you **post** a letter, you put a stamp on it and send it to someone.
ટપાલમાં રવાના

poster *noun*
posters

A **poster** is a large notice or picture that you stick on a wall.
ભીંત પર ચોડવામાં આવતી નોટિસ, જાહેરખબર કે મોટું ચિત્ર

potato *noun*
potatoes

Potatoes are hard round white vegetables with brown or red skins. They grow under the ground.
બટેટા

a b c d e f g h i j k l m n o **p** q r s t u v w x y z

103

pour *verb*
pours, pouring, poured

If you **pour** something like water, you make it flow out of a container.
રેડવું

powder *noun*

Powder is a fine dry dust, like flour.
ભૂકો, ચૂરો

power *noun*

1   If someone has **power**, they have control over people.
અધિકાર, સત્તા
*He has the **power** to keep you in after school.*

2   The **power** of something is its strength.
ક્રિયાશક્તિ, ક્ષમતા
*The engine doesn't often work at full **power**.*

practise *verb*
practises, practising, practised

If you **practise** something, you do it often in order to do it better.
આદત પાડવી
*I've been **practising** my song.*

present *noun*
presents

1   The **present** is the period of time that is taking place now.
વર્તમાનકાળ

2   A **present** is something that you give to someone for them to keep.
ભેટ, દેણગી
*She got a **present** for her birthday.*

present *adjective*

If someone is **present** somewhere, they are there.
ઉપસ્થિત
*He wasn't **present** when they called out his name.*

press *verb*
presses, pressing, pressed

If you **press** something, you push it hard.
દબાવવું
Press the blue button.

pretend *verb*
pretends, pretending, pretended

When you **pretend**, you act as if something is true, when you know it isn't.
ડોળ કરવો
*She **pretended** to be the teacher.*

pretty *adjective*
prettier, prettiest

If something is **pretty**, it is nice to look at.
સુંદર
*She was wearing a **pretty** necklace.*

price *noun*
prices

The **price** of something is how much you have to pay to buy it.
કિંમત
*Could you tell me the **price** of this car, please?*

prick *verb*
pricks, pricking, pricked

If you **prick** something, you stick something sharp like a pin or a knife into it.
ઘોંચવું કે ભોંકવું
*She **pricked** her finger on a pin.*

prince *noun*
princes

A **prince** is a boy or a man in the family of a king or queen.
રાજકુમાર

princess *noun*
princesses

A **princess** is a girl or a woman in the family of a king or queen.
રાજકુમારી

print *verb*
prints, printing, printed

1 If you **print** something, you use a machine to put words or pictures on paper.
ચિત્ર ઇ. છાપવું

2 If you **print** when you are writing, you do not join the letters together.
છુટા અક્ષરે લખવું

prison *noun*
prisons

A **prison** is a building where people who have broken the law are kept as a punishment.
જેલ

*He was sent to **prison** for five years.*

prize *noun*
prizes

A **prize** is money or a special thing that you give to the person who wins a game, a race, or a competition.
ઇનામ

*He won first **prize**.*

problem *noun*
problems

A **problem** is something or someone that makes thing difficult, or that makes you worry.
મુશ્કેલી, સમસ્યા, કોયડો

program *noun*
programs

A **program** is a set of instructions that a computer uses to do a job.
કમ્પ્યૂટર પ્રોગ્રામ

programme *noun*
programmes

A **programme** is a television or radio show.
ટેલીવિઝન કે રેડિયો કાર્યક્રમ
*She is watching her favourite television **programme**.*

project *noun*
projects

A **project** is a plan that takes a lot of time and effort.
પરિયોજના

*It was a large building **project**.*

promise *verb*
promises, promising, promised

If you **promise** to do something, you say that you will be sure to do it.
વચન કે ખાતરી આપવી

*I **promise** that I'll help you all I can.*

pronoun *noun*
pronouns

A **pronoun** is a word that you use in place of a noun when you are talking about someone or something. "It" and "she" are **pronouns**.
સર્વનામ

proper *adjective*

The **proper** thing or way is the one that is right.
યોગ્ય

*Put things in their **proper** place.*

protect *verb*
protects, protecting, protected

If you **protect** something, you keep it safe.
રક્ષા કરવી

*Make sure you **protect** your skin from the sun.*

proud *adjective*
prouder, proudest

If you feel **proud**, you feel pleased about something good that you or other people close to you have done.
ગર્વ

*I was **proud** of our team today.*

pudding *noun*
puddings

A **pudding** is something sweet that you eat after your main meal.
શીરા જેવી એક ગળી વાની

*We had a delicious chocolate **pudding**.*

a b c d e f g h i j k l m n o p q r s t u v w x y z

105

puddle *noun*
puddles

A **puddle** is a small amount of water on the ground.
ખાબોચિયું
*Splashing in **puddles** is lots of fun.*

pull *verb*
pulls, pulling, pulled

When you **pull** something, you hold it and move it towards you.
ખેંચવું
*The dentist had to **pull** out all his teeth.*

punishment *noun*
punishments

Punishment is something done to someone because they have done something wrong.
સજા
*His father sent him to bed early as a **punishment** for being rude.*

pupil *noun*
pupils

The **pupils** at a school are the children who go there.
વિદ્યાર્થી, શિષ્ય
*Around 200 **pupils** go to this school.*

puppet *noun*
puppets

A **puppet** is a small model of a person or animal that you can move.
કઠપૂતળી

puppy *noun*
puppies

A **puppy** is a young dog.
કુરકુરિયું

purple *noun*

Purple is a mixture of red and blue.
જાંબુડિયા રંગનું
*Some grapes are **purple**.*

purse *noun*
purses

A **purse** is a small bag that women use to carry money and other things.
બટવો
*She reached in her **purse** for her money.*

push *verb*
pushes, pushing, pushed

When you **push** something, you press it in order to move it away from you.
ધક્કો મારવો
*I **pushed** back my chair and stood up.*

put *verb*
puts, putting, put

When you **put** something somewhere, you move it there.
મૂકવું
*He **put** the book on the desk.*

puzzle *verb*
puzzles, puzzling, puzzled

If something **puzzles** you, you do not understand it and you feel confused.
સમસ્યા, કોયડો
*There was something about her that **puzzled** me.*

pyjamas *noun*

Pyjamas are loose trousers and a jacket that you wear in bed.
પાયજામો

pyramid *noun*
pyramids

A **pyramid** is a solid shape with a flat base and flat sides that make a point where they meet at the top.
પિરામિડ

A B C D E F G H I J K L M N O P Q R S T U V W X Y Z

quack *verb*
quacks, quacking, quacked

When a duck **quacks**, it makes a loud sound.
બતકનો કર્કશ અવાજ
*There were ducks **quacking** on the lawn.*

quarrel *noun*
quarrels

A **quarrel** is an angry argument between people.
કજિયો, ઝઘડો, તકરાર
*I had an awful **quarrel** with my brothers.*

quarter *noun*
quarters

A **quarter** is one of four equal parts of something.
પા- ચોથા ભાગનું
*My sister ate a **quarter** of the chocolate cake.*

queen *noun*
queens

A **queen** is a woman who rules a country, or a woman who is married to a king.
રાણી
*The crowd cheered when the **queen** went past.*

question *noun*
questions

A **question** is something that you say or write to ask a person about something.
પ્રશ્ન, સવાલ
*They asked her a lot of **questions** about her holiday.*

queue *noun*
queues

A **queue** is a line of people or cars waiting for something.
હાર કે કતાર(લોકોની)
*He stood in the lunch **queue** for ten minutes.*

quick *adjective*
quicker, quickest

Something that is **quick** moves or does things with great speed.
ઝડપી
*The cat was so **quick** that I couldn't catch it.*

quickly

If you move or do something **quickly** you do it with great speed.
ઝડપથી
*The girl ran **quickly** along the street.*

quiet *adjective*
quieter, quietest

Someone who is **quiet** makes only a small amount of noise or no noise at all.
શાંત
*The baby was so **quiet** I didn't know he was there.*

quite

Quite means a bit but not a lot.
સર્વથા, તદ્દન, સાવ
*I **quite** like her but she's not my best friend.*

quiz *noun*
quizzes

A **quiz** is a game in which someone asks you questions to find out what you know.
પ્રશ્ન હરીફાઈ
*After dinner we had a TV **quiz** and our team won.*

a b c d e f g h i j k l m n o p q r s t u v w x y z

rabbit noun
rabbits

A **rabbit** is a small animal with long ears. **Rabbits** live in holes in the ground.
સસલું
*The children were excited when they heard they were getting a pet **rabbit**.*

race noun
races

A **race** is a competition to see who is fastest, for example in running or driving.
રેસ, હરીફાઈ
*Nobody can beat my sister in a **race**.*

radiator noun
radiators

A **radiator** is a metal thing filled with hot water or steam. **Radiators** keep rooms warm.
રેડિયેટર - ઉષ્ણતા પ્રસારક યંત્ર
*I burned myself on the **radiator** in the bathroom.*

radio noun
radios

A **radio** is a piece of equipment you use to hear programmes with talking, news and music.
રેડિયો
*Turn on the **radio** for the news please.*

railway noun
railways

A **railway** is a special road for trains, with stations along it. **Railways** have two metal lines that are always the same distance apart.
રેલમાર્ગ
*The house was beside the **railway**.*

rain noun

Rain is water that falls from the clouds in small drops.
વરસાદ
*My mother told me not to go out in the **rain**.*

rainbow noun
rainbows

A **rainbow** is a half circle of different colours in the sky. You can sometimes see a **rainbow** when it rains.
મેઘધનુષ
*A **rainbow** appeared when the storm was over.*

ran

⇨ Look at **run**.
*I **ran** to school because I was late.*

rang

⇨ Look at **ring**.
*I got worried when the phone **rang**.*

rare adjective
rarer, rarest

Something that is **rare** is not seen or heard very often.
વિરલ, જવલ્લે
*We are lucky to see this bird because it is very **rare**.*

raspberry noun
raspberries

A **raspberry** is a small soft red fruit. **Raspberries** grow on bushes.
રાસ્બરી- લાલ રસાળ ફળ
*Would you like some **raspberries** with your ice cream?*

rat noun
rats

A **rat** is an animal that looks like a mouse. A **rat** has a long tail and sharp teeth.
ઉંદર
*The old house was full of **rats**.*

rather

You use **rather** to mean "a little bit".
કેટલેક અંશે
*I thought the party was **rather** boring.*

raw *adjective*

Raw food has not been cooked.
રાંધ્યા વિનાનું, કાચું
*There is a bowl of **raw** carrots and cauliflower on the table.*

reach *verb*

reaches, reaching, reached

1 When you **reach** a place, you arrive there.
(આવી કે જઈ) પહોંચવું
*We will not **reach** home until midnight.*

2 If you **reach** somewhere, you move your arm and hand to take or touch something.
હાથ લાંબો કરીને લેવું કે અડકવું
*I **reached** into my bag and brought out a pen.*

read *verb*

reads, reading, read

When you **read**, you look at written words and understand them, and sometimes say them aloud.
વાંચવું
*My father **reads** me a story every night before I go to sleep.*

ready *adjective*

If you are **ready**, you are able to do something or go somewhere right now.
તૈયાર
*It takes her a long time to get **ready** for school.*

real *adjective*

1 Something that is **real** is true and is not imagined.
સાચું
*No, it wasn't a dream. It was **real**.*

2 If something is **real**, it is not a copy.
કૃત્રિમ નહિ, અસલ
*Is your necklace **real** gold?*

really

1 You say **really** to show how much you mean something.
ખરેખર, સાચે જ,
*I'm **really** sorry I can't come to your party.*

2 You say **really** to show that what you are saying is true.
ચોક્કસ
*Are we **really** going to the zoo?*

reason *noun*

reasons

The **reason** for something is the fact which explains why it happens.
કારણ
*You must have a good **reason** for being so late.*

receive *verb*

receives, receiving, received

When you **receive** something, someone gives it to you, or you get it after it has been sent to you.
લેવું, મેળવવું, સ્વિકારવું
*Did you **receive** the birthday card I sent you?*

recipe *noun*

recipes

A **recipe** is a list of food and a set of instructions telling you how to cook something.
વાનગી બનાવવાની રીત
*Do you have a **recipe** for chocolate cake?*

recite *verb*

recites, reciting, recited

When someone **recites** a poem or other piece of writing, they say it aloud after they have learned it.
મુખપાઠ કરેલું બોલવું કે ગાવું
*We each had to **recite** a poem in front of the class.*

record *noun*

records

A **record** is the best result ever.
વિક્રમ
*What's the world **record** for the 100 metres?*

record *verb*

records, recording, recorded

If you **record** something like a TV programme, you make a copy of it so that you can watch it later.
ફિલ્મ ઉતારવી
*Can you **record** the football for me please?*

recorder *noun*

recorders

A **recorder** is a small instrument in the shape of a pipe. You play a **recorder** by blowing into it and putting your fingers over the holes in it.
એક જાતનો પાવો
*He has been learning the **recorder** for three years.*

rectangle *noun*
rectangles

A **rectangle** is a shape with four straight sides.
લંબચોરસ

red *noun*

Red is the colour of blood or a strawberry.
લાલ
*Her dress is bright **red**.*

reflection *noun*
reflections

A **reflection** is something you can see on a smooth, shiny surface. What you see is really in a different place.
પ્રતિબિંબ

***Reflections** always show things the wrong way round.*

refuse *verb*
refuses, refusing, refused

If you **refuse** to do something, you say that you will not do it.
ના પાડવી
*He **refuses** to have a bath.*

remember *verb*
remembers, remembering, remembered

If you **remember** people or things from the past, you can bring them into your mind and think about them.
યાદ રાખવું કે હોવું
*I **remember** the first time I met him.*

remind *verb*
reminds, reminding, reminded

If someone **reminds** you about something, they help you to remember it.
યાદ દેવડાવવું, -નું ધ્યાન દોરવું
***Remind** me to buy a bottle of milk, will you?*

remove *verb*
removes, removing, removed

If you **remove** something from a place, you take it away.
કાઢી નાખવું
*When the cake is cooked, **remove** it from the oven.*

repair *verb*
repairs, repairing, repaired

If you **repair** something that is damaged or broken, you fix it so that it works again.
મરામત કરવી
*The man managed to **repair** the broken tap.*

repeat *verb*
repeats, repeating, repeated

If you **repeat** something, you say it, write it, or do it again.
ફરી બોલવું, ફરી કરવું
*Please can you **repeat** the question?*

reply *verb*
replies, replying, replied

If you **reply** to something, you say or write an answer.
જવાબ આપવો
*Will you please **reply** when I ask you a question.*

reptile *noun*
reptiles

A **reptile** is an animal that has cold blood, rough skin, and lays eggs. Snakes and lizards are **reptiles**.
સરિસૃપ- જમીન પર પેટેથી ઘસડાઇને ચાલનાર પ્રાણી

rescue *verb*
rescues, rescuing, rescued

If you **rescue** someone, you help them get away from a dangerous place.
ભય કે મુશ્કેલીમાં થી બચાવવું
*The police **rescued** 20 people from the roof of the building.*

rest *verb*
rests, resting, rested

If you **rest**, you sit or lie down and do not do anything active for a while.
આરામ કરવો
*My grandmother always **rests** in the afternoon.*

A B C D E F G H I J K L M N O P Q **R** S T U V W X Y Z

rest *noun*

The **rest** is the parts of something that are left.
બાકીનું
*Who ate the **rest** of the cake?*

restaurant *noun*
restaurants

A **restaurant** is a place where you can buy and eat a meal.
ભોજનાલય
*We had lunch in an Italian **restaurant**.*

result *noun*
results

A **result** is something that happens because another thing has happened.
પરિણામ
*I got measles and as a **result** was off school for two weeks.*

return *verb*
returns, returning, returned

1 When you **return** to a place, you go back to it after you have been away.
   પાછા જવું
   *He **returned** to Japan after his holiday in England.*

2 If you **return** something to someone, you give it back to them.
   પરત કરવું, પાછું આપવું
   *I forgot to **return** my library books.*

reward *noun*
rewards

A **reward** is something that is given to a person because they have done something good.
ઇનામ
*The school gives **rewards** to children who behave well.*

rhinoceros *noun*
rhinoceroses

A **rhinoceros** is a large wild animal with thick grey skin. A **rhinoceros** has one or two horns on its nose.
ગેંડો

rhyme *verb*
rhymes, rhyming, rhymed

If two words **rhyme**, they have the same sound at the end of them.
અનુપ્રાસ મળતા કરવા, જોડકણાં કરવાં
*Sally **rhymes** with valley.*

rhythm *noun*
rhythms

Rhythm is something which is repeated again and again in the same way.
તાલ
*Listen to the **rhythm** of the music.*

rib *noun*
ribs

Your **ribs** are the 12 pairs of curved bones that go round your body.
પાંસળી
*He fell off his bike and broke a **rib**.*

ribbon *noun*
ribbons

A **ribbon** is a long narrow piece of cloth. You use **ribbons** to decorate things or tie them together.
રેશમી કે સુતરાઉ ફિત કે પટ્ટી
*The girl's hair was tied with a blue and white **ribbon**.*

rice *noun*

Rice is white or brown grains from a plant. **Rice** grows in wet areas.
ચોખા
*The meal was chicken, **rice**, and vegetables.*

rich *adjective*
richer, richest

Someone who is **rich** has a lot of money and expensive things.
ધનવાન
*She is a **rich** woman who owns a very large house.*

riddle *noun*
riddles

A **riddle** is a question that seems to be nonsense, but that has a clever answer.
ઉખાણું
*He asked the **riddle**, "What key cannot open a door?" and I answered, "a monkey".*

a
b
c
d
e
f
g
h
i
j
k
l
m
n
o
p
q
r
s
t
u
v
w
x
y
z

A B C D E F G H I J K L M N O P Q **R** S T U V W X Y Z

ride *verb*
rides, riding, rode, ridden
When you **ride** a horse or a bike, you sit on it and control it as it moves along.
સવારી કરવી
*The girl **rode** her horse along the beach.*

right *adjective*
1 If something is **right**, it is correct and there have been no mistakes.
બરોબર, સાચું
*Only one child in the class knew the **right** answer to the teacher's question.*
2 The **right** side is the side that is towards the east when you look north.
જમણું
*Most people write with their **right** hand.*

ring *verb*
rings, ringing, rang, rung
When a bell **rings**, it makes a clear, loud sound.
વાગવું
*The school bell **rings** at nine o'clock.*

ring *noun*
rings
A **ring** is a round piece of metal that you wear on a finger.
વીંટી, અંગૂઠી
*He turned the **ring** on his finger.*

ripe *adjective*
riper, ripest
When fruit or grain is **ripe**, it is ready to be eaten.
પાકું
*Don't eat the apples until they are **ripe**.*

rise *verb*
rises, rising, rose, risen
If something **rises**, it moves up.
ઊંચે ચડવું કે ઊઠવું
*We watched the balloon **rise** into the sky.*

river *noun*
rivers
A **river** is a long line of water that flows into the sea.
નદી

*The Nile is one of the longest **rivers** in the world.*

road *noun*
roads
A **road** is a long piece of hard ground for vehicles to travel on.
રસ્તો

*You must look both ways before you cross the **road**.*

roar *verb*
roars, roaring, roared
If a person, an animal or a thing **roars**, they make a very loud noise.
ગરજવું
*The engines **roared** and the aeroplane started to move.*

robot *noun*
robots
A **robot** is a machine that can move and do things that it has been told to do.
રોબોટ - યંત્ર માનવ

*We have **robots** that we could send to the moon.*

rock *noun*
rocks
1 **Rock** is the hard material that is in the ground and in mountains.
ખડક
*We tried to dig, but the ground was solid **rock**.*
2 A **rock** is a piece of this material.
પથ્થર
*She picked up a **rock** and threw it into the lake.*

rock *verb*
rocks, rocking, rocked
If something **rocks**, it moves from side to side.
હીંડોળવું, આમતેમ ડોલવું

rocket *noun*
rockets
A **rocket** is a vehicle that people use to travel into space.
રોકેટ, લાંબી નળી જેવું અંતરિક્ષનું વાહન
*This is the **rocket** that took them to the moon.*

rode
⇨ Look at **ride**.
*The man **rode** his bike down the hill.*

roll *verb*
rolls, rolling, rolled

When something **rolls**, it moves along a surface, turning over and over.
ગબડવું
*The ball bounced out of the garden and **rolled** across the road.*

roof *noun*
roofs

The **roof** of a building is the bit on top that covers it.
છાપરું
*Our house is the one with the red **roof**.*

room *noun*
rooms

1 A **room** is a part of a building that has its own walls.
ઓરડો
*A minute later he left the **room**.*

2 If there is **room** somewhere, there is a enough empty space.
ખાલી જગ્યા
*There isn't **room** for any more furniture in here.*

root *noun*
roots

The **roots** of a plant are the parts of it that grow under the ground.
મૂળ
*She dug a hole near the **roots** of an apple tree.*

rope *noun*
ropes

A **rope** is a type of very thick string that is made by twisting together several strings or wires.
દોરડું
*He tied the **rope** around his waist.*

rose *noun*
roses

A **rose** is a large garden flower with a lovely smell. **Roses** grow on bushes.
ગુલાબ
*The teacher was given a bunch of red **roses**.*

rough *adjective*
rougher, roughest

1 If something is **rough**, it is not smooth or even.
ખરબચડું
*His hands were **rough**.*

2 If you are **rough**, you are not being careful or gentle.
કઠોર
*Don't be so **rough** or you'll break it.*

round *adjective*
rounder, roundest

Something **round** is in the shape of a ball or a circle.
ગોળ
*There was a **round** table in the middle of the room.*

row *noun*
rows

A **row** is a line of things or people.
હાર, પંક્તિ
*Our house is opposite a **row** of shops.*

rub *verb*
rubs, rubbing, rubbed

If you **rub** something, you move your hand or a cloth backwards and forwards over it.
ઘસવું
*I **rubbed** the window and looked outside.*

rubber *noun*
rubbers

1 **Rubber** is a strong material that stretches. **Rubber** is used to make things like tyres and boots for wet weather.
રબર

2 A **rubber** is a small piece of rubber used to remove pencil mistakes.
પેન્સિલથી લખેલું છેકવાનું રબર
*Have you got a **rubber** in your pencil case? she's*

A B C D E F G H I J K L M N O P Q R S T U V W X Y Z

rubbish *noun*

Rubbish is things like empty packs and used paper that you throw away.
કચરો, નકામી ચીજ

rude *adjective*
ruder, rudest

If people are **rude**, they are not polite.
ઉદ્ધત

*It is **rude** to ask for something without saying "please".*

ruin *verb*
ruins, ruining, ruined

If you **ruin** something, you destroy or spoil it.
વિનાશ કરવો

*The rain **ruined** the party.*

rule *noun*
rules

Rules are instructions that tell you what you must do or must not do.
નિયમ

*Can you explain the **rules** of cricket to me?*

rule *verb*
rules, ruling, ruled

Someone who **rules** a country controls it.
રાજ કરવું

ruler *noun*
rulers

1 A **ruler** is a long, flat piece of wood or plastic with straight edges. You use a **ruler** for measuring things or drawing straight lines.
આંકણી

2 A **ruler** is also a person who rules a country.
રાજકર્તા
   *He was **ruler** of France at that time.*

run *verb*
runs, running, ran, run

When you **run**, you move very quickly on your legs.
દોડવું

*It's very dangerous to **run** across the road.*

rung
➩ Look at **ring**.
*They had **rung** the door bell when I was in the shower.*

sad *adjective*
sadder, saddest

If you are **sad**, you don't feel happy.
દુ:ખી

*I'm **sad** that he is leaving.*

safe *adjective*
safer, safest

If you are **safe**, you are not in any danger.
સલામત

*Is it **safe**?*

said
➩ Look at **say**.
*That is what she **said** to me.*

sail *noun*
sails

Sails are large pieces of cloth on a boat that catch the wind and move the boat along.
સઢ

salad *noun*
salads

A **salad** is a mixture of vegetables and sometimes other foods. You usually eat **salads** cold.
કચુંબર

salt *noun*

Salt is a white powder that you use to make food taste better.
મીઠું-લવણ

*Now add **salt** and pepper.*

same *adjective*

If two things are the **same**, they are like one another.
એકસરખું
*The two cats look the **same**.*

sand *noun*

Sand is a powder made of very small pieces of stone. Deserts and most beaches are made of **sand**.
રેતી

sandal *noun*
sandals

Sandals are light shoes that you wear in warm weather.
સેન્ડલ- એક પ્રકારનાં પગરખાં

*He put on a pair of old **sandals**.*

sandwich *noun*
sandwiches

A **sandwich** is two slices of bread with another food such as cheese or meat between them.
સેન્ડવિચ

*She ate a large **sandwich**.*

sang

➪ Look at **sing**.
*She **sang** a happy song.*

sank

➪ Look at **sink**.
*The boat **sank** in the storm.*

sari *noun*
saris

A **sari** is a long piece of material worn folded around the body by women.
સાડી

*She was wearing a new yellow **sari**.*

sat

➪ Look at **sit**.
*She **sat** down next to the fire.*

satellite *noun*
satellites

A **satellite** is a machine that is sent into space to receive and send back information.
ઉપગ્રહ

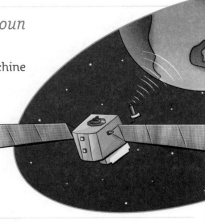

Saturday *noun*
Saturdays

Saturday is the day after Friday and before Sunday.
શનિવાર

*He called her on **Saturday** morning.*

saucepan *noun*
saucepans

A **saucepan** is a deep metal container with a long handle and a lid. **Saucepans** are used for cooking.
કડાઇ

*Put the potatoes in a **saucepan** and boil them.*

saucer *noun*
saucers

A **saucer** is a small curved plate that you put under a cup.
રકાબી

a b c d e f g h i j k l m n o p q r **s** t u v w x y z

A B C D E F G H I J K L M N O P Q R S T U V W X Y Z

sausage noun
sausages

A **sausage** is a mixture of very small pieces of meat and other foods, inside a long thin skin.
ઝીણા આંતરડાના કકડામાં મસાલા સાથે

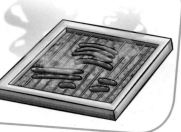

save verb
saves, saving, saved

1 If you **save** someone or something, you help them to escape from danger.
બચાવવું
He **saved** the boy from drowning.

2 If you **save** something, you keep it because you will need it later.
બચત કરવી
She was **saving** her money.

saw
⇒ Look at **see**.
We **saw** her walking down the street.

saw noun
saws

A **saw** is a metal tool for cutting wood.
કરવત
He used a **saw** to cut the branches off the tree.

say verb
says, saying, said

When you **say** something, you talk.
કહેવું
She **said** that they were very pleased.

scale noun
scales

Scales are small, flat pieces of hard skin that cover the body of animals like fish and snakes.
ભીંગડું

scales noun
Scales are a machine used for weighing things.
ત્રાજવું
He weighed flour on the **scales**.

scared adjective

If you are **scared** of something it frightens you.
ડરવું
She is **scared** of spiders.

school noun
schools

A **school** is a place where people go to learn.
વિદ્યાલય
The **school** was built in the 1960s.

science noun
sciences

Science is the study of natural things.
વિજ્ઞાન

scissors noun

Scissors are a small tool for cutting with two sharp parts that are joined together.
કાતર
Cut the card using **scissors**.

score verb
scores, scoring, scored

If you **score** in a game, you get a goal, run, or point.
રમનારે જીતેલા દાવ
He **scored** his second goal of the game.

scratch verb
scratches, scratching, scratched

1 If a sharp thing **scratches** someone or something, it makes small cuts on their skin or on its surface.
ઉઝરડા પાડવા
The branches **scratched** my face.

2 If you **scratch** part of your body, you rub your nails against your skin.
ખંજવાળવું
He **scratched** his head.

scream verb
screams, screaming, screamed

If you **scream**, you shout or cry in a loud, high voice.
ચીસ પાડવી
She **screamed** when she saw the spider.

116

screen *noun*

screens

A **screen** is a flat surface on which a picture is shown.
સિનેમા ઇ.નાં ચિત્રો બતાવવાનો પડદો
*There was dust on the television **screen**.*

sea *noun*

seas

A **sea** is a large area of salt water.
દરિયો
*They swam in the warm **sea**.*

seal *verb*

seals, sealing, sealed

When you **seal** an envelope, you close it by folding part of it and sticking it down.
ઉઘડે નહિ એવી રીતે બંધ કરવું
*He **sealed** the envelope and put on a stamp.*

search *verb*

searches, searching, searched

If you **search** for something or someone, you look for them everywhere.
શોધ
*I am **searching** for my glasses.*

seaside *noun*

The **seaside** is an area next to the sea.
દરિયાકાંઠાનો વિસ્તાર
*I went to spend a few days at the **seaside**.*

season *noun*

seasons

The **seasons** are the four parts of a year: spring, summer, autumn and winter.
ઋતુ
*Spring is my favourite **season**.*

seat *noun*

seats

A **seat** is something that you can sit on.
બેઠક

second *adjective*

The **second** thing in a number of things is the one that you count as number two.
બીજું, પહેલા પછીનું
*It was the **second** day of his holiday.*

second *noun*

seconds

A **second** is an amount of time. There are sixty **seconds** in one minute.
મિનિટનો સાઠમો ભાગ, સેકંડ
*For a few **seconds** nobody spoke.*

secret *adjective*

If something is **secret**, only a small number of people know about it, and they do not tell any other people.
ગુપ્ત, ગૂઢ
*He knew a **secret** place to hide in the garden.*

see *verb*

sees, seeing, saw, seen

1 If you **see** something, you are looking at it or you notice it.
જોવું
*The fog was so thick we couldn't **see** anything.*

2 If you **see** someone, you meet them.
મળવું
*I **saw** him yesterday.*

seed *noun*

seeds

A **seed** is the small, hard part of a plant from which a new plant grows.
બીજ
*Plant the **seeds** in the garden.*

seem *verb*

seems, seeming, seemed

If something **seems** to be true, it appears to be true or you think it is true.
લાગવું
*The thunder **seemed** very close.*

a
b
c
d
e
f
g
h
i
j
k
l
m
n
o
p
q
r
s
t
u
v
w
x
y
z

seen

⇒ Look at **see**.

*She had **seen** the film before.*

sell *verb*
sells, selling, sold

If you **sell** something, you let someone have it in return for money.

વેચવું

*The man **sold** his bike.*

semicircle *noun*
semicircles

A **semicircle** is a half of a circle, or something with this shape.

અર્ધગોળાકાર

*The children stood in a **semicircle**.*

send *verb*
sends, sending, sent

When you **send** someone a message or a parcel, you make it go to them.

મોકલવું

*I will **send** you a letter when I arrive.*

sensible *adjective*

If you do something **sensible**, you have thought about it a lot first.

સમજદાર

*The **sensible** thing is not to touch it.*

sent

⇒ Look at **send**.

*He **sent** a letter home.*

September *noun*

September is the month after August and before October. It has 30 days.

સપ્ટેમ્બર મહિનો

serve *verb*
serves, serving, served

Someone who **serves** customers in a shop or a restaurant helps them with what they want to buy.

પીરસવું

*She **served** me coffee and pie.*

set *noun*
sets

A **set** of things is a number of things that belong together.

ચીજોનો સમૂહ

*I'll need a **set** of clean clothes.*

seven

Seven is the number **7**.

સાત

several *adjective*

You use **several** for talking about a number of people or things that is not large but is greater than two.

કેટલાક

*There were **several** boxes on the table.*

sew *verb*
sews, sewing, sewed, sewn

When you **sew** pieces of cloth together, you join them using a needle and thread.

સિલાઇ કરવી, સીવવું

*I must **sew** a button on to this shirt.*

sex *noun*
sexes

The **sex** of a person or animal is if it is male or female.

લિંગભેદ

*What **sex** is the baby?*

shadow *noun*
shadows

A **shadow** is a dark shape on a surface that is made when something blocks the light.
પડછાયો
*The **shadows** of the trees crossed their path.*

shake *verb*
shakes, shaking, shook, shaken

1 If you **shake** something, you hold it and move it quickly up and down.
હલાવવું
***Shake** the bottle before you drink.*

2 If someone or something **shakes**, they move quickly backwards and forwards or up and down.
ધ્રૂજવું, કાંપવું
*My body was **shaking** with cold.*

shallow *adjective*
shallower, shallowest

If something is **shallow**, it is not deep.
છીછરું
*The river is very **shallow** here.*

shape *noun*
shapes

The **shape** of something is the way its outside edges or surfaces look.
આકાર
*Pasta comes in different **shapes** and sizes.*

share *verb*
shares, sharing, shared

If you **share** something with another person, you both have it or use it.
ભાગ પાડવો
*We **shared** an ice cream.*

shark *noun*
sharks

A **shark** is a very large fish. **Sharks** have very sharp teeth and some may attack people.
શાર્ક - મોટી માછલી

sharp *adjective*
sharper, sharpest

1 A **sharp** point or edge is very thin and can cut through things quickly.
તીક્ષ્ણધાર કે અણીવાળું
*Be careful, the scissors are **sharp**.*

2 A **sharp** feeling is sudden and is very big or strong.
એકદમ, અચાનક
*I felt a **sharp** pain in my right leg.*

shave *verb*
shaves, shaving, shaved

If you **shave**, you remove hair from your face or body by cutting it off.
દાઢી કરવી
*Rahim took a bath and **shaved**.*

shed *noun*
sheds

A **shed** is a small building where you store things.
છાપરું
*The house has a large **shed** in the garden.*

she'd

1 **She'd** is short for **she had**.
એણે કર્યું હતું (સ્ત્રીલિંગ)
***She'd** already seen them.*

2 **She'd** is also short for **she would**.
એણે કર્યું હતું (સ્ત્રીલિંગ)
***She'd** be very happy.*

sheep *noun*
sheep

A **sheep** is a farm animal with thick hair called wool. Farmers keep **sheep** for their wool or for their meat.
ઘેટું

sheet *noun*
sheets

1 A **sheet** is a large piece of cloth that you sleep on or cover yourself with in bed.
ઓછાડ, ચાદર
*Once a week, we change the **sheets**.*

2 A **sheet** is a piece of paper, glass, plastic, or metal.
(કાગળનો) તાવ
*He folded the **sheets** of paper.*

a
b
c
d
e
f
g
h
i
j
k
l
m
n
o
p
q
r
s
t
u
v
w
x
y
z

A
B
C
D
E
F
G
H
I
J
K
L
M
N
O
P
Q
R
S
T
U
V
W
X
Y
Z

shelf *noun*
shelves

A **shelf** is a long flat piece of wood on a wall or in a cupboard that you can keep things on.
છાજલી
*Dad took a book from the **shelf**.*

shell *noun*
shells

1 The **shell** of an egg or nut is its hard part.
ઇંડું, ઇ.નું કોચલું

2 The **shell** of an animal such as a snail is the hard part that covers its back and protects it.
કાચલું, કવચ

she'll

She'll is short for **she will**.
તે કરશે (સ્ત્રીલિંગ)
***She'll** be back.*

she's

She's is short for **she is**.
તેણીનું છે, એ છે
***She's** a doctor.*

shine *verb*
shines, shining, shone

If something **shines**, it gives out bright light.
ચમકવું, પ્રકાશવું
*Today it's warm and the sun is **shining**.*

shiny *adjective*
shinier, shiniest

If something is **shiny**, it is bright.
ચમકીલું
*Her hair was **shiny** and clean.*

ship *noun*
ships

A **ship** is a large boat that carries people or things.
જહાજ
*The **ship** was ready to leave.*

shirt *noun*
shirts

A **shirt** is something you wear on the top part of your body. It has a collar and buttons.
ખમીસ

shiver *verb*
shivers, shivering, shivered

If you **shiver**, your body shakes because you are cold or scared.
થથરવું
*She **shivered** with cold.*

shoe *noun*
shoes

Shoes are a type of clothing that you wear on your feet.
પગરખાં
*I need a new pair of **shoes**.*

shone

⇨ Look at **shine**.
*The sun **shone** all day.*

shop *noun*
shops

A **shop** is a place that sells things.
દુકાન
*He and his wife run a clothes **shop**.*

shore *noun*
shores

The **shore** of a sea or lake is the land along the edge of it.
કિનારો
*They walked slowly down to the **shore**.*

short *adjective*
shorter, shortest

1 If something is **short**, it does not last very long.
ટૂંકું
*Last year we all went to the seaside for a **short** holiday.*

2 A **short** thing is small in length, distance, or height.
ઠીંગણું (ઊંચું નહિ)
*She has **short**, straight hair.*

shorts *noun*

Shorts are trousers with short legs.
અર્ધ પાટલૂન, ચડ્ડી
*He was wearing blue **shorts**.*

should *verb*

You use **should** when you are saying what is the right thing to do.
સંભવિત કે અપેક્ષિત ઘટના અથવા સંકેતાર્થ વ્યક્ત કરનારું
*He **should** tell us what happened.*

shoulder *noun*
shoulders

Your **shoulders** are the two parts of your body between your neck and the tops of your arms.
ખભો
*Put your hands on the **shoulders** of the person in front of you.*

shout *verb*
shouts, shouting, shouted

If you **shout**, you say something in a very loud voice.
ઘાટો પાડીને કે
*He **shouted** something to his brother.*

show *verb*
shows, showing, showed, shown

1 If you **show** someone something, you let them see it.
બતાવવું
*She **showed** me her ring.*

2 If you **show** someone how to do something, you teach them how to do it.
કરી બતાવવું, સમજાવવું
*She **showed** us how to make pasta.*

shower *noun*
showers

1 A **shower** is a thing that you stand under, that covers you with water so you can wash yourself.
ઉપરથી ઝરીમાંથી પાણી પડવું
*I was in the **shower** when the phone rang.*

2 A **shower** is a short period of rain.
વરસાદ
*A few **showers** are expected tomorrow.*

shown

⇨ Look at **show**.
*I've **shown** them how to do it.*

shut *verb*
shuts, shutting, shut

If you **shut** something, you close it.
બંધ કરવું
*Please **shut** the gate.*

shy *adjective*
shyer, shyest

If you are **shy**, you are nervous about talking to people that you do not know well.
શરમાળ
*She was a **shy**, quiet girl.*

sick *adjective*
sicker, sickest

If you are **sick**, you are not well.
માંદું
*He's very **sick** and needs a doctor.*

side *noun*
sides

1 The **side** of something is a place to the left or right of it.
બાજુ, તરફ
*On the left **side** of the door there's a door bell.*

2 The **side** of something is also its edge.
બાજુ
*A square has four **sides**.*

3 The different **sides** in a game are the groups of people who are playing against each other.
સામો પક્ષ
*Both **sides** want to win the match.*

a
b
c
d
e
f
g
h
i
j
k
l
m
n
o
p
q
r
s
t
u
v
w
x
y
z

A
B
C
D
E
F
G
H
I
J
K
L
M
N
O
P
Q
R
S
T
U
V
W
X
Y
Z

sign *noun*
signs

1 A **sign** is a mark or a shape that has a special meaning.
ચિહ્ન
*In maths, **+** is a plus **sign** and **-** is a minus **sign**.*

2 You can also make a **sign** to somebody by moving something.
ઈશારો
*They gave me a **sign** to show that everything was all right.*

silent *adjective*

1 If you are **silent**, you are not talking.
અબોલ
*She was **silent** because she did not know what to say.*

2 If something is **silent**, it is quiet, with no sound at all.
શાંત
*The room was **silent**.*

silly *adjective*
sillier, silliest

If you are **silly**, you do not behave in a sensible way.
મૂર્ખ
*Don't be **silly**!*

silver *noun*

Silver is a valuable metal.
ચાંદી
*He bought her a bracelet made from **silver**.*

sing *verb*
sings, singing, sang, sung

When you **sing**, you make music with your voice.
ગાવું
*I love **singing**.*

sink *noun*
sinks

A **sink** is a large fixed container in a kitchen or a bathroom that you can fill with water.
કૂંડી
*The **sink** was filled with dirty dishes.*

sister *noun*
sisters

Your **sister** is a girl or woman who has the same parents as you.
બહેન
*This is my **sister**.*

sit *verb*
sits, sitting, sat

If you are **sitting** in a chair, your bottom is resting on the chair and the top part of your body is straight.
બેસવું
*Mum was **sitting** in her chair in the kitchen.*

six

Six is the number .
છ ની સંખ્યા

size *noun*
sizes

The **size** of something is how big or small it is.
માપ, કદ
*The **size** of the room is about five metres by seven metres.*

skate *noun*
skates

Skates are boots with a thin metal bar on the bottom for moving quickly on ice.
બરફ પર સરકવા માટે તળિયે લોહની પટ્ટીવાળા પગરખાં

skeleton *noun*
skeletons

A **skeleton** is all the bones in a person's or animal's body.
હાડપિંજર
*A human **skeleton** has more than 200 bones.*

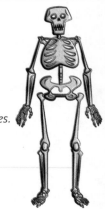

skies

⇨ Look at **sky**.
*The **skies** were grey.*

skill noun

If you have **skill** you are able to do something well.
કુશળતા

*He shows great **skill** on the football field.*

skin noun
skins

1 Your **skin** covers your whole body.
ચામડી
*Too much sun can damage your **skin**.*

2 The **skin** of a fruit or vegetable covers the outside of it.
છાલ
*She slipped on a banana **skin**.*

skip verb
skips, skipping, skipped

1 If you **skip** along, you move along jumping from one foot to the other.
છલાંગો મારતાં ચાલવું
*We **skipped** down the street.*

2 If you **skip** something, you decide not to do it.
ટાળવું
*Don't **skip** breakfast.*

skirt noun
skirts

A **skirt** is something that women and girls wear. It hangs down from the waist and covers part of the legs.
સ્કર્ટ, સ્ત્રીને પહેરવાનો ઘેર કે ધાઘરો

skull noun
skulls

A person's or animal's **skull** is the bones of their head.
ખોપરી
*Your **skull** protects your brain.*

sky noun
skies

The **sky** is the space around the Earth which you can see when you look up.
આકાશ
*The sun was shining in the **sky**.*

sleep verb
sleeps, sleeping, slept

If you **sleep**, you rest with your eyes closed and you do not move.
નિંદર
*Be quiet! The baby is **sleeping**.*

sleeve noun
sleeves

The **sleeves** of something you wear are the parts that cover your arms.
બાંય
*She wore a blue dress with long **sleeves**.*

slept

⇨ Look at **sleep**.
*She **slept** for three hours.*

slice noun
slices

A **slice** of something is a thin piece that you cut from a larger piece.
પાતળી કકડો
*Would you like a **slice** of bread?*

slide verb
slides, sliding, slid

When someone or something **slides**, they move quickly over a surface.
સરકવું
*She **slid** across the ice on her stomach.*

slip verb
slips, slipping, slipped

If you **slip**, you slide and fall.
લપસવું
*He **slipped** on the wet grass.*

slipper noun
slippers

Slippers are loose, soft shoes that you wear indoors.
સ્લિપર, નરમ ખુલ્લા જોડા
*She put on a pair of **slippers**.*

a
b
c
d
e
f
g
h
i
j
k
l
m
n
o
p
q
r
s
t
u
v
w
x
y
z

slippery *adjective*

If something is **slippery**, it is smooth or wet, and is difficult to walk on or to hold.

લપસણું

*Be careful—the floor is **slippery**.*

slope *noun*
slopes

A **slope** is the side of a mountain, hill, or valley.

ઢોળાવ

*A steep **slope** leads to the beach.*

slow *adjective*
slower, slowest

If something is **slow**, it does not move quickly.

ધીમું

*The bus was very **slow**.*

slowly

If something moves **slowly**, it does not move quickly.

ધીમેથી

slug *noun*
slugs

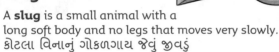

A **slug** is a small animal with a long soft body and no legs that moves very slowly.

કોટલા વિનાનું ગોકળગાય જેવું જીવડું

small *adjective*
smaller, smallest

If something is **small**, it is not large in size or amount.

નાનું

*She is **small** for her age.*

smash *verb*
smashes, smashing, smashed

If you **smash** something, it breaks into many pieces.

ભાંગીને ભૂક્કો થવો

*The plate **smashed** when it hit the floor.*

smell *noun*
smells

The **smell** of something is what you notice about it when you breathe in through your nose.

ગંધ

*There was a horrible **smell** in the fridge.*

smile *verb*
smiles, smiling, smiled

If you **smile**, the corners of your mouth turn up because you are happy or you think that something is funny.

મલકાટ, સ્મિત, મંદ હાસ્ય

*He **smiled** at me.*

smoke *noun*

Smoke is the black or white clouds of gas that you see in the air when something burns.

ધુમાડો

*Thick black **smoke** blew over the city.*

smooth *adjective*
smoother, smoothest

Something **smooth** has no rough parts, lumps, or holes.

સમતલ, સપાટ

*The baby's skin was soft and **smooth**.*

snail *noun*
snails

A **snail** is a small animal with a long, soft body, no legs, and a round shell on its back.

ગોકળગાય

snake *noun*
snakes

A **snake** is a long, thin animal with no legs, that slides along the ground.

સાપ

sneeze *verb*
sneezes, sneezing, sneezed

When you **sneeze**, you suddenly take in air and then blow it down your nose in a noisy way.

છીંક ખાવી

*Cover your nose and mouth when you **sneeze**.*

snow *noun*

Snow is pieces of soft white frozen water that fall from the sky.
બરફ

*Six inches of **snow** fell last night.*

soap *noun*

Soap is something that you use with water for washing yourself.
સાબુ

*She bought a bar of **soap**.*

sock *noun*
socks

Socks are pieces of cloth that you wear over your foot and ankle, inside your shoes.
પગના મોજા

*I have a pair of red **socks**.*

sofa *noun*
sofas

A **sofa** is a long, comfortable seat with a back, that two or three people can sit on.
સોફા

soft *adjective*
softer, softest

1 Something that is **soft** is nice to touch, and not rough or hard.
નરમ, પોચું
*She wiped the baby's face with a **soft** cloth.*

2 A **soft** sound or light is very gentle.
હળવું,
*There was a **soft** tapping on my door.*

soil *noun*

Soil is the top layer on the surface of the earth in which plants grow.
જમીન

*The **soil** here is good for growing vegetables.*

sold

⇨ Look at **sell**.

*They **sold** their house today.*

soldier *noun*
soldiers

A **soldier** is someone who is in an army.
સૈનિક

solid *adjective*

1 Something that is **solid** stays the same shape if it is in a container or not.
કઠણ, ઘટ્ટ

2 Something that is **solid** is not hollow.
નક્કર મજબુત
*They had to cut through 5 feet of **solid** rock.*

some

You use **some** to talk about an amount of something.
થોડુંક, કેટલુંક
*Can I have **some** orange juice please?*

somebody

You use **somebody** to talk about a person without saying who you mean.
કોઈ એક

someone

You use **someone** to talk about a person without saying who you mean.
કોઈ એક

*I need **someone** to help me.*

something

You use **something** to talk about a thing without saying what it is.
કંઈક

*He knew that there was **something** wrong.*

sometimes

You use **sometimes** to talk about things that do not take place all the time.
ક્યારેક

***Sometimes** he's a little rude.*

somewhere

You use **somewhere** to talk about a place without saying where you mean.
કોઇક જગ્યાએ
*I've seen him before **somewhere**.*

son *noun*
sons

Someone's **son** is their male child.
દીકરો
*His **son** is seven years old.*

song *noun*
songs

A **song** is words and music sung together.
ગીત
*She sang a **song**.*

soon *adjective*
sooner, soonest

If you are going to do something **soon** you will do it a very short time from now.
થોડીવારમાં
*I'll call you **soon**.*

sore *adjective*
sorer, sorest

If part of your body is **sore**, it is painful.
દુખતું
*I had a **sore** throat.*

sorry *adjective*
sorrier, sorriest

1   If you are **sorry** about something, you feel sad about it.
દિલગીર
*I'm **sorry** he's gone.*

2   If you feel **sorry** for someone, you feel sad for them.
દુઃખી કે વ્યથિત
*I felt **sorry** for him because nobody listened to him.*

sort *noun*
sorts

The different **sorts** of something are the different types of it.
જાત, વર્ગ, શ્રેણી
*What **sort** of school do you go to?*

sound *noun*
sounds

A **sound** is something that you hear.
અવાજ
*He heard the **sound** of a car engine outside.*

soup *noun*

Soup is liquid food made by boiling meat, fish, or vegetables in water.
સૂપ

sour *adjective*

Something that is **sour** has a sharp, nasty taste.
ખાટું
*Lemons have a **sour** taste.*

south *noun*

The **south** is the direction to your right when you are looking towards the place where the sun rises.
દક્ષિણ દિશા

space *noun*
spaces

1   You use **space** to talk about an area that is empty.
ખાલી જગ્યા
*They cut down trees to make **space** for houses.*

2   **Space** is the area past the Earth, where the stars and planets are.
અંતરિક્ષ, અવકાશ
*The six astronauts will spend ten days in **space**.*

spade *noun*
spades

A **spade** is a tool that is used for digging.
પાવડો

speak *verb*
speaks, speaking, spoken

When you **speak**, you say words.
બોલવું
*He **spoke** in a whisper.*

A B C D E F G H I J K L M N O P Q R S T U V W X Y Z

special *adjective*

Someone or something that is **special** is better or more important than other people or things.
વિશેષ

*Mum made a **special** cake for my birthday.*

speed *noun*
speeds

The **speed** of something is how fast it moves or is done.
ઝડપ

*He drove off at high **speed**.*

spell *verb*
spells, spelling, spelled or spelt

When you **spell** a word, you write or say each letter in the correct order.
ઉચ્ચારવું

*He **spelled** his name.*

spend *verb*
spends, spending, spent

1 When you **spend** money, you buy things with it.
(પૈસા) ખરચવું, વાપરવું
*I have **spent** all my money.*

2 To **spend** time or energy is to use it doing something.
સમય પસાર કરવો
*She **spends** hours working on her garden.*

spider *noun*
spiders

A **spider** is a small animal with eight legs.
કરોળિયો

spill *verb*
spills, spilling, spilled or spilt

If you **spill** a liquid, you make it flow over the edge of a container by accident.
ઢોળવું કે ઢોળાવું

*He always **spilled** the drinks.*

spin *verb*
spins, spinning, spun

If something **spins**, it turns around quickly.
ગોળ ગોળ ફરવું કે ભમવું

*He made the coin **spin** on his desk.*

spine *noun*
spines

Your **spine** is the row of bones down your back.
કરોડ

splash *verb*
splashes, splashing, splashed

If you **splash** in water, you hit the water in a noisy way.
પાણી છપછપ કરવું

*The children **splashed** around in the water.*

spoil *verb*
spoils, spoiling, spoiled or spoilt

1 If you **spoil** something, you damage it or stop it from working as it should.
બગાડવું
*Don't **spoil** the surprise.*

2 If you **spoil** children, you give them everything they want or ask for.
લાડ લડાવીને કે પંપાળીને બગાડવું
*She acted like a **spoilt** child.*

a
b
c
d
e
f
g
h
i
j
k
l
m
n
o
p
q
r
s
t
u
v
w
x
y
z

A
B
C
D
E
F
G
H
I
J
K
L
M
N
O
P
Q
R
S
T
U
V
W
X
Y
Z

spoke noun
spokes

The **spokes** of a wheel are the bars which join the outside ring to the centre.
આરો

spoke
⇨ Look at **speak**.
*She **spoke** in a loud voice.*

spoken
⇨ Look at **speak**.
*He has **spoken** to us.*

spoon noun
spoons

A **spoon** is a long tool with a round end that is used for eating, serving or mixing food.
ચમચો
*He stirred his coffee with a **spoon**.*

sport noun
sports

Sports are games which need energy and skill.
રમતગમત
*She is very good at **sport**.*

spot noun
spots

Spots are small, round areas on a surface.
ડાઘો,ટપકું
*The leaves are yellow with orange **spots**.*

spot verb
spots, spotting, spotted

If you **spot** something or someone, you notice them.
જણાવું કે જાણવામાં આવવું
*I didn't **spot** the mistake in his work.*

spout noun
spouts

A **spout** is a tube for pouring liquid.
નાળયું
*My kettle has a long **spout**.*

spray noun
sprays

Spray is a lot of small drops of water that are thrown into the air.
છંટકાવ, છાંટ, ફરફર
*The **spray** from the waves covered them.*

spread verb
spreads, spreading, spread

1 If you **spread** something somewhere, you open it out.
પાથરવું,બિછાવવું
*She **spread** a towel on the sand and lay on it.*

2 If you **spread** something on a surface, you put it all over the surface.
ચોપડવું
*She was **spreading** butter on the bread.*

3 If something **spreads**, it reaches a larger area.
ફેલાવું
*The news **spread** quickly.*

spring noun
springs

1 **Spring** is the season between winter and summer when the weather becomes warmer and plants start to grow again.
વસંતઋતુ
*They are getting married next **spring**.*

2 A **spring** is a long piece of metal that goes round and round. It goes back to the same shape after you pull it.
કમાન, સ્પ્રિંગ
*The **springs** in the bed were old.*

spun
⇨ Look at **spin**.
*He **spun** the wheel.*

square noun
squares

A **square** is a shape with four straight sides that are all the same length.
ચોરસ
*Cut the cake in **squares**.*

squirrel noun
squirrels

A **squirrel** is a small animal with a long thick tail. **Squirrels** live in trees.
ખિસકોલી

stable *noun*
stables

A **stable** is a building where people keep horses.
તબેલો

stairs *noun*

Stairs are steps you walk down or up in a building.
સીડી
*He walked up the **stairs**.*

stamp *noun*
stamps

A **stamp** is a small piece of paper that you stick on an envelope before you post it.
ટપાલની ટિકિટ
*She put a **stamp** on the corner of the envelope.*

stamp *verb*
stamps, stamping, stamped

If you **stamp** your foot, you put your foot down very hard on the ground.
પછાડવું
*I **stamped** my feet to keep warm.*

stand *verb*
stands, standing, stood

When you are **standing**, you are on your feet.
ઊભા રહેવું
*She was **standing** beside my bed.*

star *noun*
stars

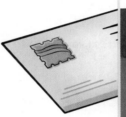

1 A **star** is a large ball of burning gas in space. **Stars** look like small points of light in the sky.
તારો
Stars lit the sky.

2 A **star** is a shape that has four, five, or more points sticking out of it in a pattern.
તારાના જેવી નિશાની કે ફૂદડી (*)
*How many **stars** are there on the flag?*

3 A **star** is somebody who is famous for doing something, for example acting or singing.
મુખ્ય નટ કે નટી
*He's one of the **stars** of a TV show.*

start *verb*
starts, starting, started

1 When something **starts**, it begins.
શરૂ થવું
*When does the film **start**?*

2 If you **start** to do something, you begin to do it.
શરૂ કરવું
*She **started** to read her book.*

station *noun*
stations

A **station** is a place where trains or buses stop so that people can get on or off.
સ્ટેશન- મથક
*We went to the train **station**.*

stay *verb*
stays, staying, stayed

1 If you **stay** in a place, you do not move away from it.
ટકી રહેવું
*She **stayed** in bed until noon.*

2 If you **stay** somewhere, you live there for a short time.
રોકાવું કે મુકામ કરવો
*He **stayed** with them for two weeks.*

steady *adjective*
steadier, steadiest

Something that is **steady** is firm and not shaking.
અચલ, અવિચલ
*He held out a **steady** hand.*

steal *verb*
steals, stealing, stole, stolen

If you **steal** something from someone, you take it without asking or telling them and don't give it back.
ચોરવું
*They said he **stole** a bicycle.*

A
B
C
D
E
F
G
H
I
J
K
L
M
N
O
P
Q
R
S
T
U
V
W
X
Y
Z

steam *noun*

Steam is the hot gas that water becomes when it boils.
વરાળ
*The **steam** rose into the air.*

steel *noun*

Steel is a very strong metal that is made from iron.
પોલાદ
*The door is made of **steel**.*

steep *adjective*
steeper, steepest

A **steep** slope rises quickly and is difficult to go up.
ઊભાં ચઢાણવાળું
*Some of the hills are very **steep**.*

stem *noun*
stems

The **stem** of a plant is the long, thin part that the flowers and leaves grow on.
દાંડી
*He cut the **stem** and gave her the flower.*

step *noun*
steps

1 If you take a **step**, you lift your foot and put it down in a different place.
પગલું
*I took a **step** towards him.*

2 A **step** is a flat surface that you put your feet on to walk up or down to somewhere.
પગથિયું
*We went down the **steps** into the garden.*

stick *noun*
sticks

A **stick** is a long, thin piece of wood.
લાકડી
*She put some dry **sticks** on the fire.*

stick *verb*
sticks, sticking, stuck

If you **stick** one thing to another, you join them together using glue.
ચોંટાડવું
*Now **stick** your picture on a piece of paper.*

stiff *adjective*
stiffer, stiffest

Something that is **stiff** is firm and is not easy to bend.
અક્કડ
*The sheet of cardboard was **stiff**.*

still *adjective*
stiller, stillest

If you are **still**, you are not moving.
સ્થિર
*Please stand **still**.*

sting *verb*
stings, stinging, stung

If a plant, an animal, or an insect **stings** you, a part of it is pushed into your skin so that you feel a sharp pain.
ડંખ મારવો
*She was **stung** by a bee.*

stir *verb*
stirs, stirring, stirred

When you **stir** a liquid, you move it around using a spoon or a stick.
હલાવવું

stole

⇨ Look at **steal**.
*They **stole** our car last night.*

stolen

⇨ Look at **steal**.
*All of her money was **stolen**.*

stomach noun
stomachs

Your **stomach** is the place inside your body where food goes when you eat it.
પેટ

*His **stomach** felt full after the meal.*

stone noun
stones

1 **Stone** is a hard solid material that is found in the ground. It is often used for building.
પથ્થર

*The floor was solid **stone**.*

2 A **stone** is a small piece of rock that is found on the ground.
કાંકરી

*He took a **stone** out of his shoe.*

stood

⇨ Look at **stand**.

*He **stood** in the street.*

stop verb
stops, stopping, stopped

1 If you **stop** doing something, you do not do it any more.
રોકવું

***Stop** throwing those stones!*

2 If something **stops**, it does not do what it did any more.
બંધ થવું કે અટકવું

*The rain has **stopped**.*

store verb
stores, storing, stored

If you **store** something, you keep it somewhere safe.
સંગ્રહ કરવો

storm noun
storms

A **storm** is very bad weather, with heavy rain and strong winds.
તોફાન

*There will be **storms** along the East Coast.*

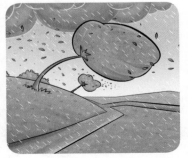

story noun
stories

When someone tells you a **story** they describe people and things that are not real, in a way that makes you enjoy hearing about them.
વાર્તા

*I'm going to tell you a **story** about four little rabbits.*

straight adjective
straighter, straightest

If something is **straight**, it goes one way and does not bend.
સીધું

*The boat moved in a **straight** line.*

strange adjective
stranger, strangest

Something that is **strange** is unusual.
વિચિત્ર

*I had a **strange** dream last night.*

straw noun
straws

1 **Straw** is the dry, yellow stems of crops.
સૂકું ઘાસ, પરાળ
*The floor of the barn was covered with **straw**.*

2 A **straw** is a thin tube that you use to suck a drink into your mouth.
પીણું પીવાની સાંકડી નળી
*I drank my milk through a **straw**.*

strawberry noun
strawberries

A **strawberry** is a small soft red fruit that has a lot of very small seeds on its skin.
સ્ટ્રોબેરી- લાલ રંગનું નાનું ફળ

stream noun
streams

A **stream** is a small narrow river.
ઝરણું

*There was a **stream** at the end of the garden.*

A B C D E F G H I J K L M N O P Q R S T U V W X Y Z

street *noun*
streets

A **street** is a road in a city or a town.
શેરી

*The **streets** were full of people.*

strength *noun*

Your **strength** is how strong you are.
તાકાત

*Swimming builds up the **strength** of your muscles.*

stretch *verb*
stretches, stretching, stretched

1 Something that **stretches** over an area covers all of it.
પાથરેલું હોવું
*The line of cars **stretched** for miles.*

2 When you **stretch**, you hold out part of your body as far as you can.
તાણવું, ખેંચવું
*He yawned and **stretched**.*

strict *adjective*
stricter, strictest

A **strict** person expects people to obey rules.
કડક
*My parents are very **strict**.*

string *noun*
strings

1 **String** is thin rope that is made of twisted threads.
દોરી
*He held out a small bag tied with **string**.*

2 The **strings** on an instrument are the thin pieces of wire that are stretched across it and that make sounds when the instrument is played.
તાર
*He changed a guitar **string**.*

strip *noun*
strips

A **strip** of something is a long, narrow piece of it.
પાતળી પટ્ટી

*Cut a **strip** off a piece of paper, then twist it and stick the two ends together. Then cut it along the middle and see what happens.*

stripe *noun*
stripes

A **stripe** is a long line that is a different colour from the areas next to it.
જુદા રંગનો પટો

*She wore a blue skirt with white **stripes**.*

strong *adjective*
stronger, strongest

1 Someone who is **strong** is healthy with good muscles.
સશક્ત
*I'm not **strong** enough to carry him.*

2 **Strong** things are not easy to break.
મજબૂત,
*This **strong** plastic will not crack.*

stuck *adjective*

1 If something is **stuck** in a place, it cannot move.
ફસાવું
*His car got **stuck** in the snow.*

2 If you get **stuck**, you can't go on doing something because it is too difficult.
જરૂરીયાતવાળું
*The teacher will help if you get **stuck**.*

stung

⇨ Look at **sting**.
*He was **stung** by a wasp.*

submarine *noun*
submarines

A **submarine** is a ship that can travel under the sea.
સબમરીન

subtraction *noun*

Subtraction is when you take one number away from another.
બાદબાકી

suck *verb*
sucks, sucking, sucked

If you **suck** something, you hold it in your mouth for a long time.
ચૂસવું
*They **sucked** their sweets.*

sudden *adjective*

Something **sudden** is quick and is not expected.
અણધાર્યું
*The car came to a **sudden** stop.*

suddenly

Suddenly is quickly, without being expected.
અચાનક
***Suddenly** there was a loud bang.*

sugar *noun*

Sugar is a sweet thing that is used for making food and drinks taste sweet.
ખાંડ
*Do you take **sugar** in your coffee?*

suit *noun*
suits

A **suit** is a jacket and trousers or a skirt that are made from the same cloth.
એકબીજા સાથે મેળખાય એવા કપડાંની જોડ
*He was wearing a dark **suit**.*

sum *noun*
sums

1 A **sum** of money is an amount of money.
કૂલ રકમ
*Large **sums** of money were lost.*

2 In maths, a **sum** is a problem you work out using numbers.
ગણિતનો દાખલો
*I have to finish these **sums**.*

summer *noun*
summers

Summer is the season after spring and before autumn. In the **summer** the weather is usually warm or hot.
ઉનાળો

sun *noun*
suns

The **sun** is the large ball of burning gas in the sky that gives us light.
સૂર્ય
*The **sun** was now high in the sky.*

Sunday *noun*
Sundays

Sunday is the day after Saturday and before Monday.
રવિવાર
*We went for a drive on **Sunday**.*

sunflower *noun*
sunflowers

A **sunflower** is a very tall plant with large yellow flowers.
સૂરજમુખી

sung

⇨ Look at **sing**.
*She has **sung** the song many times before.*

sunk

⇨ Look at **sink**.
*The rock has **sunk** to the bottom of the river.*

sunny *adjective*
sunnier, sunniest

When it is **sunny**, the sun is shining.
તડકાવાળું
*The weather was warm and **sunny**.*

a b c d e f g h i j k l m n o p q r s t u v w x y z

A B C D E F G H I J K L M N O P Q R S T U V W X Y Z

sunshine *noun*

Sunshine is the light that comes from the sun.
તડકો
*She was sitting outside in bright **sunshine**.*

supermarket *noun*
supermarkets

A **supermarket** is a large shop that sells all kinds of food and other things for the home.
સુપરબજાર, બધી ચીજો વેચતું મોટું બજાર
*Lots of people buy food in a **supermarket**.*

sure *adjective*

If you are **sure** that something is true, you know that it is true.
ચોક્કસ
*I am **sure** my answer is correct.*

surface *noun*
surfaces

The **surface** of something is the flat top part of it or the outside of it.
સપાટી
*There were pen marks on the table's **surface**.*

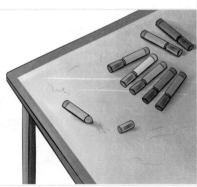

surname *noun*
surnames

Your **surname** is your last name which you share with other people in your family.
અટક

surprise *noun*
surprises

A **surprise** is something that you do not expect.
અચંબો, નવાઈ, આશ્ચર્ય
*I have a **surprise** for you!*

swallow *verb*
swallows, swallowing, swallowed

If you **swallow** something, you make it go from your mouth down into your stomach.
ગળી જવું
*She took a bite of the apple and **swallowed** it.*

swam

⇨ Look at **swim**.
*She **swam** across the river.*

swan *noun*
swans

A **swan** is a large bird with a long neck, that lives on rivers and lakes.
(રાજ) હંસ

sweep *verb*
sweeps, sweeping, swept

If you **sweep** an area, you push dirt off it using a brush with a long handle.
સાફ કરવું
*The man in the shop was **sweeping** the floor.*

sweet *adjective*
sweeter, sweetest

Sweet food and drink has a lot of sugar in it.
ગળ્યું, મીઠું
*Mum gave me a cup of **sweet** tea.*

sweet *noun*
sweets

Sweets are foods that have a lot of sugar.
મીઠાઈ
*Don't eat too many **sweets**.*

swept

➡️ Look at **sweep**.

*The rubbish was **swept** away.*

swim *verb*
swims, swimming, swam, swum

When you **swim**, you move through water by moving your arms and legs.
તરવું

*She learned to **swim** when she was three.*

swing *verb*
swings, swinging, swung

If something **swings**, it keeps moving backwards and forwards or from side to side through the air.
ઝુલાવવું

*She walked beside him with her arms **swinging**.*

switch *noun*
switches

A **switch** is a small button for turning something on or off.
વીજળીના ઉપકરણો ચાલુ બંધ કરવાનું બટન

*She pressed the **switch** to turn on the light.*

sword *noun*
swords

A **sword** is like a long knife, with a handle and a long sharp blade.
તલવાર

swum

➡️ Look at **swim**.

*He had never **swum** so far.*

swung

➡️ Look at **swing**.

*She **swung** her bag backwards and forwards.*

table *noun*
tables

A **table** is a piece of furniture that has legs and a flat top.
મેજ, ટેબલ

tadpole *noun*
tadpoles

A **tadpole** is a small black animal with a round head and a long tail that lives in water. **Tadpoles** grow into frogs or toads.
દેડકાનું બચ્ચું

tail *noun*
tails

An animal's **tail** is the long, thin part at the end of its body.
પૂંછડી

take *verb*
takes, taking, took, taken

1 If you **take** something, you move it or carry it.
   સાથે લઈ જવું
   *She **took** the plates into the kitchen.*

2 If you **take** something that does not belong to you, you steal it.
   કોઈનું કશુંક લઈ લેવું કે ઝૂંટવી લેવું
   *Someone **took** all our money.*

3 If you **take** a vehicle, you ride in it from one place to another.
   પકડવું
   *We **took** the bus to school.*

talk *verb*
talks, talking, talked

When you **talk**, you say things to someone.
વાત કરવી

*She **talked** to him on the phone.*

a
b
c
d
e
f
g
h
i
j
k
l
m
n
o
p
q
r
s
t
u
v
w
x
y
z

A
B
C
D
E
F
G
H
I
J
K
L
M
N
O
P
Q
R
S
T
U
V
W
X
Y
Z

tall *adjective*
taller, tallest

If a person or thing is **tall**, they are higher than usual from top to bottom.
ઊંચું
*It was a very **tall** building.*

tame *adjective*
tamer, tamest

If an animal or bird is **tame**, it is not afraid of people and will not try to hurt them.
પાળેલું

tap *verb*
taps, tapping, tapped

If you **tap** something, you hit it but you do not use a lot of strength.
ટકોરો મારવો
*He **tapped** on the door and went in.*

tape *noun*

Tape is a long, thin strip of plastic that has glue on one side. You use **tape** to stick things together.
ચોટાડવાની સાંકડી પટ્ટી
*He wrapped the parcel with paper and **tape**.*

taste *verb*
tastes, tasting, tasted

If you **taste** something, you eat or drink a small amount of it to see what it is like.
ચાખવું, ચાખી જોવું
*She **tasted** the soup and then added some salt.*

taught

⇨ Look at **teach**.
*My mum **taught** me to read.*

tea *noun*

1 **Tea** is a drink. You make it by pouring hot water on to the dry leaves of a plant called the **tea** bush.
ચા

2 **Tea** is also a meal that you eat in the afternoon or the early evening.
ચા સાથેનો હળવો નાસ્તો

teach *verb*
teaches, teaching, taught

If you **teach** someone something, you help them to understand it or you show them how to do it.
શીખવવું
*He **teaches** people how to play the piano.*

teacher *noun*
teachers

A **teacher** is a person whose job is to teach other people. **Teachers** usually work in schools.
શિક્ષક

team *noun*
teams

A **team** is a group of people who work together, or who play a sport together against another group.
ટીમ- ટુકડી
*He is in the school football **team**.*

tear *noun*
tears

Tears are the liquid that comes out of your eyes when you cry.
આંસું, અશ્રુ
*Her face was wet with **tears**.*

tear *verb*
tears, tearing, tore, torn

If you **tear** something, you pull it into pieces or make a hole in it.
ફાડવું, ચીરવું
*Try not to **tear** the paper.*

teeth

⇨ Look at **tooth**.

*Clean your **teeth** before you go to bed.*

telephone *noun*
telephones

A **telephone** is a machine that you use to talk to someone who is in another place.
ટેલીફોન

television *noun*
televisions

A **television** is a machine that shows moving pictures with sound on a screen.
દૂરદર્શન

tell *verb*
tells, telling, told

1 If you **tell** someone something, you let them know about it.
જણાવવું
Tell me about your holiday.

2 If you **tell** someone to do something, you say that they must do it.
કહેવું
She told me to go away.

3 If you can **tell** something, you know it.
ખાતરી કરવી
I can tell that he is angry.

ten *noun*

Ten is the number .
દસ

tent *noun*
tents

A **tent** is made of strong material that is held up with long pieces of metal and ropes. You sleep in a **tent** when you stay in a camp.
તંબુ

term *noun*
terms

A **term** is one of the parts of a school year. There are usually three **terms** in a year.
મર્યાદિત અવધિ, શાળા ઈ.નું સત્ર, ટર્મ

terrible *adjective*

If something is **terrible**, it is very bad.
અત્યંત ખરાબ
That was a terrible film.

test *verb*
tests, testing, tested

If you **test** something, you try it to see what it is like, or how it works.
પરીક્ષા કરવી, કસોટી કરવી
Test the water to see if it is warm.

test *noun*
tests

A **test** is something you do to show how much you know or what you can do.
પરીક્ષા, કસોટી
The teacher gave us a maths test.

thank *verb*
thanks, thanking, thanked

When you **thank** someone, you tell them that you are pleased about something they have given you or have done for you. You usually do this by saying "Thank you".
આભાર માનવો
I thanked him for my present.

theatre *noun*
theatres

A **theatre** is a building where you go to see people acting stories, singing, or dancing.
નાટ્યગૃહ

a
b
c
d
e
f
g
h
i
j
k
l
m
n
o
p
q
r
s
t
u
v
w
x
y
z

their

You use **their** to say that something belongs to a group of people, animals, or things.
તેમનું, તેઓનું
*They took off **their** coats.*

theirs

You use **theirs** to say that something belongs to a group of people, animals, or things.
તેમનું, તેઓનું
*The house next to **theirs** was empty.*

then

1 **Then** means at that time.
તે વખતે
*He wasn't as rich **then** as he is now.*

2 You also use **then** to say that one thing happens after another.
તે પછી, બાદ
*She said good night, **then** went to bed.*

there

1 You use **there** to say that something is in a place or is happening, or to make someone notice it.
ત્યાં
There are flowers on the table.

2 **There** also means to a place, or at a place.
તે જગ્યાએ, તે સ્થળે
*I have never been **there** before.*

there's

There's is short for **there is**.
છે
There's nothing in the box.

they

You use **they** when you are talking about more than one person, animal, or thing.
તેઓ
***They** are all in the same class.*

they'd

1 **They'd** is short for **they had**.
તેમણે કર્યું હતું

2 **They'd** is also short for **they would**.
તેમણે કર્યું હતું
*The boys said **they'd** come back later.*

they'll

They'll is short for **they will**.
તેઓ કરશે
***They'll** be here on Monday.*

they're

They're is short for **they are**.
તેઓ છે
***They're** going to the circus.*

they've

They've is short for **they have**.
તેમણે કર્યું છે
***They've** gone away.*

thick *adjective*
thicker, thickest

1 If something is **thick**, it is deep or wide between one side and the other.
જાડું
*He cut a **thick** slice of bread.*

2 If a liquid is **thick**, it flows slowly.
ગાઢું, ઘાટું
*This soup is very **thick**.*

thigh *noun*
thighs

Your **thighs** are the parts of your legs that are above your knees.
જાંઘ
*His **thighs** ached from climbing the hill.*

thin *adjective*
thinner, thinnest

1 If something is **thin**, it is narrow between one side and the other.
બારીક, પાતળું
*The book is printed on very **thin** paper.*

2 If a person or animal is **thin**, they are not fat and they do not weigh much.
પાતળું, ઝીણું
*He was a tall, **thin** man.*

thing *noun*
things

A **thing** is something that is not a plant, an animal, or a human being.
ચીજ, વસ્તુ
*What's that **thing** lying in the road?*

think *verb*
thinks, thinking, thought

1 If you **think** something, you believe that it is true.
લાગવું, ધારવું
*I **think** it's a great idea.*

2 When you **think**, you use your mind.
વિચારવું, વિચાર કરવો
*I tried to **think** what to do.*

thirsty *adjective*
thirstier, thirstiest

If you are **thirsty**, you want to drink something.
તરસ્યું

thought
⇒ Look at **think**.
*I **thought** they were here.*

thread *noun*
threads

Thread is a long, thin piece of cotton or wool that you use to sew cloth.
દોરો

three *noun*
Three is the number **3**.
ત્રણ

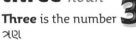

threw
⇒ Look at **throw**.
*She **threw** her coat on to a chair.*

throat *noun*
throats

1 Your **throat** is the back part of your mouth that you use to swallow and to breathe.
ગળું

2 Your **throat** is also the front part of your neck.
ગરદનનો આગળનો ભાગ

through

Through means going all the way from one side of something to the other side.
આરપાર
*We walked **through** the forest.*

throw *verb*
throws, throwing, threw, thrown

When you **throw** something you are holding, you move your hand quickly and let the thing go, so that it moves through the air.
ફેંકવું
***Throw** the ball to me.*

thumb *noun*
thumbs

Your **thumb** is the short, thick finger on the side of your hand.
અંગૂઠો
*The baby sucked its **thumb**.*

thunder *noun*

Thunder is the loud noise that you sometimes hear from the sky when there is a storm.
ગડગડાટ

Thursday *noun*
Thursdays

Thursday is the day after Wednesday and before Friday.
ગુરુવાર
*I saw her on **Thursday**.*

a b c d e f g h i j k l m n o p q r s t u v w x y z

A
B
C
D
E
F
G
H
I
J
K
L
M
N
O
P
Q
R
S
T
U
V
W
X
Y
Z

tidy *adjective*
tidier, tidiest
Something that is **tidy** is neat, with everything in its proper place.
સુઘડ

tie *verb*
ties, tying, tied
If you **tie** something, you fasten it with string or a rope.
બાંધવું
*He **tied** the dog to the fence.*

tie *noun*
ties
A **tie** is a long, narrow piece of cloth that you tie a knot in and wear around your neck with a shirt.
ગળાપટ્ટી, નેકટાઇ

tiger *noun*
tigers
A **tiger** is a large wild cat that has orange fur with black stripes.
વાઘ

tight *adjective*
tighter, tightest
1   If clothes are **tight**, they are so small that they fit very close to your body.
તંગ, સાંકડું
*His trousers were very **tight**.*

2   Something that is **tight** is fastened so that it is not easy to move it.
સજ્જડ
*The string was tied in a **tight** knot.*

time *noun*
1   **Time** is how long something takes to happen. We measure **time** in minutes, hours, days, weeks, months, and years.
કાળ
*I've known him for a long **time**.*

2   The **time** is a moment in the day that you describe in hours and minutes.
સમય, વખત
*"What **time** is it?"—"Ten past five."*

tin *noun*
tins
1   **Tin** is a kind of soft, pale grey metal.
કલાઈ(ની ધાતુ),

2   A **tin** is a metal container for food.
ટિન, ટિનનો ડબ્બો
*She opened a **tin** of beans.*

tiny *adjective*
tinier, tiniest
If something is **tiny**, it is very small.
ખૂબ નાનું
*Our new kitten is **tiny**.*

tired *adjective*
If you are **tired**, you need to rest or get some sleep.
થાકેલું

toad *noun*
toads
A **toad** is a small animal that looks like a frog. **Toads** have rough, dry skin and live on land.
દેડકા જેવું પ્રાણી

today
Today means the day that is happening now.
આજે
*I feel much better **today**.*

toe *noun*
toes
Your **toes** are the five parts at the end of each foot.
પગની આંગળી
*I'm sorry I stood on your **toes**.*

together
If people do something **together**, they do it with each other.
એકબીજાની સાથે
*We played football **together**.*

told

⇨ Look at **tell**.

*We **told** them the answer.*

tomato *noun*
tomatoes

A **tomato** is a soft red fruit with a lot of juice.
ટામેટું

tomorrow

Tomorrow is the day after today.
આવતી કાલ

*I'll see you **tomorrow**.*

tongue *noun*
tongues

Your **tongue** is the soft part inside your mouth that moves when you eat or talk.
જીભ

tonight

Tonight is the evening or night that will come at the end of today.
આજ રાત

*We're going out **tonight**.*

too

1 **Too** means also.
વળી

*Can I come **too**?*

2 You also use **too** to mean more than you want or need.
અતિ

*The TV is **too** loud.*

took

⇨ Look at **take**.

*It **took** me hours.*

tool *noun*
tools

A **tool** is something that you hold in your hands and use to do a job.
સાધન

tooth *noun*
teeth

1 Your **teeth** are the hard, white things in your mouth that you use to bite and chew food.
દાંત

*I clean my **teeth** twice a day.*

2 The **teeth** of a comb, a saw, or a zip are the parts that are in a row along its edge.
કાંસકી ઇ.નો દાંતો

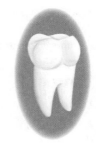

top *noun*
tops

1 The **top** of something is the highest part of it.
ટોચ

*We climbed to the **top** of the hill.*

2 The **top** of something is also the part that fits over the end of it.
ઢાંકણું

*He took the **top** off the jar.*

tore

⇨ Look at **tear**.

*She **tore** her dress on a nail.*

torn

⇨ Look at **tear**.

*He has **torn** the cover of the book.*

tortoise *noun*
tortoises

A **tortoise** is an animal with a hard shell on its back. It can pull its head and legs inside the shell. **Tortoises** move very slowly.
કાચબો

touch *verb*
touches, touching, touched

1 If you **touch** something, you put your fingers or your hand on it.
સ્પર્શ કરવો

*The baby **touched** my face.*

2 If one thing **touches** another, they are so close that there is no space between them.
અડકવું

*Her feet **touched** the floor.*

a
b
c
d
e
f
g
h
i
j
k
l
m
n
o
p
q
r
s
t
u
v
w
x
y
z

towards

Towards means in the direction of something.
...ની તરફ
*He moved **towards** the door.*

towel *noun*
towels

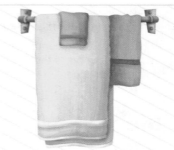

A **towel** is a piece of thick, soft cloth that you use to get yourself dry.
ટુવાલ

town *noun*
towns

A **town** is a place with a lot of streets, buildings, and shops, where people live and work.
નગર

toy *noun*
toys

A **toy** is something that you play with.
રમકડું

tractor *noun*
tractors

A **tractor** is a vehicle with big wheels at the back. **Tractors** are used on a farm to pull machines and other heavy things.
યાંત્રિક હળ, ટ્રેકટર

traffic *noun*

Traffic is all the vehicles that are on a road at the same time.
વાહનવ્યવહાર, ટ્રાફિક
*There is a lot of **traffic** in the town today.*

train *noun*
trains

A **train** is a long vehicle that is pulled by an engine along a railway line.
ટ્રેન

travel *verb*
travels, travelling, travelled

When you **travel**, you go from one place to another.
પ્રવાસ કરવો
*He **travelled** to many different countries.*

tree *noun*
trees

A **tree** is a very tall plant with branches, leaves, and a hard main part that is called a trunk.
ઝાડ

triangle *noun*
triangles

1 A **triangle** is a shape with three straight sides.
   ત્રિકોણ
2 A **triangle** is also an instrument made of metal in the shape of a **triangle** that you hit with a stick to make music.
   લોઢાના સળિયા વાળીને બનાવેલું સંગીતનું સાધન

trick *verb*
tricks, tricking, tricked

If someone **tricks** you, they make you believe something that is not true so that you will do what they want.
છેતરવું
*They **tricked** her into giving them money.*

tried

⇨ Look at **try**.
*They **tried** their best.*

tries

⇨ Look at **try**.
*She **tries** to help.*

trip *noun*
trips

When you go on a **trip**, you travel to a place and then come back.
સહેલ
*We went on a **trip** to the park.*

trousers *noun*

Trousers are things that you can wear. They cover the part of your body below the waist, and each leg.
પાટલૂન
*He was wearing brown **trousers**.*

truck *noun*
trucks

A **truck** is a large vehicle that is used to carry things.
ખટારો

true *adjective*

1 If a story is **true**, it really happened.
   સાચું
   *Everything she said was **true**.*

2 If something is **true**, it is right or correct.
   ખરું
   *Is it **true** that you have six cats?*

trunk *noun*
trunks

1 A **trunk** is the thick stem of a tree. The branches and roots grow from the **trunk**.
   ઝાડનું થડ

2 An elephant's **trunk** is its long nose. Elephants use their **trunks** to suck up water and to lift things.
   હાથીની સૂંઢ

3 A **trunk** is also a large, strong box that you use to keep things in.
   મોટી પેટી

try *verb*
tries, trying, tried

1 If you **try** to do something, you do it as well as you can.
   પ્રયત્ન કરવો
   *I will **try** to come tomorrow.*

2 If you **try** something, you test it to see what it is like or how it works.
   અજમાવી જોવું
   *Would you like to **try** my new bike?*

tube *noun*
tubes

1 A **tube** is a long, round, hollow piece of metal, rubber, or plastic.
   નળી, ભૂંગળી
   *The liquid goes through the **tube** into the bottle.*

2 A **tube** is also a soft metal or plastic container that you press to make what is in it come out.
   ટ્યૂબ
   *He bought a **tube** of glue.*

Tuesday *noun*
Tuesdays

Tuesday is the day after Monday and before Wednesday.
મંગળવાર
*He came home on **Tuesday**.*

tune *noun*
tunes

A **tune** is a piece of music that is nice to listen to.
સૂર
*She played a **tune** on the piano.*

tunnel *noun*
tunnels

A **tunnel** is a long hole that goes below the ground or through a hill.
બોગદું

A
B
C
D
E
F
G
H
I
J
K
L
M
N
O
P
Q
R
S
T
U
V
W
X
Y
Z

turn *verb*
turns, turning, turned

1 When you **turn**, you move in a different direction.
બીજી દિશામાં ફરવું
*He **turned** and walked away.*

2 When something **turns**, it moves around in a circle.
ગોળ ફરવું
*The wheels **turned** slowly.*

3 If one thing **turns** into another thing, it becomes that thing.
સ્વરૂપમાં ફેરફાર કરવો કે થવો
*The tadpole **turned** into a frog.*

4 When you **turn** a machine on, you make it start working. When you **turn** it off, you make it stop working.
બંધ બેસતું કરવું
*I **turned** off the television.*

tusk *noun*
tusks

An elephant's **tusks** are the two very long, curved teeth that it has beside its trunk.
હાથીદાંત

TV *noun*
TVs

TV is short for **television**.
ટીવી, ટેલિવિઝન
*What's on **TV**?*

twelve *noun*

Twelve is the number **12**.
બાર (એક સંખ્યા)

twice

If something happens **twice**, it happens two times.
બે વખત, બે વાર
*I've met him **twice**.*

twig *noun*
twigs

A **twig** is a very small, thin branch that grows on a tree or a bush.
ડાળખું, ઝાડની નાની ડાળી

twin *noun*
twins

If two people are **twins**, they have the same parents and they were born on the same day. **Twins** often look alike.
જોડકું, એક સાથે જન્મેલા બે બાળકો

twist *verb*
twists, twisting, twisted

If you **twist** something, you turn one end of it in one direction while you hold the other end or turn it in the opposite direction.
વળ આપવો
*She **twisted** the towel in her hands.*

two *noun*

Two is the number **2**.
બે

tying

⇨ Look at **tie**.
*He was **tying** the two pieces of rope together.*

type *noun*
types

A **type** of something is the kind of thing that it is.
પ્રકાર
*Owls are a **type** of bird.*

type *verb*
types, typing, typed

If you **type** something, you write it with a machine, for example a computer.
ટાઇપ કરવું
*She **typed** a letter.*

tyre *noun*
tyres

A **tyre** is a thick circle made of strong rubber that goes round a wheel. **Tyres** usually have air inside them.
રબરનું પૈડું

Uu

ugly *adjective*
uglier, ugliest

If something is **ugly**, it is not nice to look at.

કદરૂપું

*The monster had an **ugly** face.*

umbrella *noun*
umbrellas

An **umbrella** is a long stick that is joined to a cover made of cloth or plastic. You hold an **umbrella** over your head so that you will not get wet in the rain.

છત્રી

uncle *noun*
uncles

Your **uncle** is the brother of your mother or father, or the husband of your aunt.

કાકા, મામા, માસા, ફુવા

understand *verb*
understands, understanding, understood

If you **understand** something, you know what it means or why or how it happens.

સમજવું

*I didn't **understand** what he said.*

underwear *noun*

Your **underwear** is the name for the clothes that you wear next to your skin, under all your other clothes.

આંતરવસ્ત્ર

undress *verb*
undresses, undressing, undressed

When you **undress**, you take off your clothes.

પોતાના કપડાં ઉતારવાં, કાઢવાં

uniform *noun*
uniforms

A **uniform** is a special set of clothes that some people wear to show what job they do, or some children wear to show what school they go to.

ગણવેશ

*I put on my school **uniform**.*

until

If something happens **until** a time, it happens before that time and then stops at that time.

જ્યાં સુધી....ત્યાં સુધી નહિ

*Wait here **until** I come back.*

unusual *adjective*

If something is **unusual**, it does not happen very often.

અસામાન્ય

*It is **unusual** for him to be late.*

up

When something moves **up**, it moves from a lower place to a higher place.

ઉપર, ઉપરની જગ્યાએ

*She ran **up** the stairs.*

upon

Upon means the same as **on**.

ઉપર

*He stood **upon** the bridge.*

a b c d e f g h i j k l m n o p q r s t u v w x y z

145

upset *adjective*

If you are **upset**, you are sad because something bad has happened.
ઉદ્વિગ્ન

*I was **upset** when my brother broke my doll.*

upside down

1 If something is **upside down**, the part that is usually at the bottom is at the top.
ઊંધું

   *The picture was **upside down**.*

2 If you hang **upside down**, your head is below your feet.
ઊલટું

urgent *adjective*

If something is **urgent**, it is very important and you need to do something about it quickly.
તાકીદનું

*This problem is **urgent**.*

use *verb*
uses, using, used

If you **use** something, you do something with it.
વાપરવું

***Use** a cloth to clean the table.*

useful *adjective*

If something is **useful**, you can use it to do something or to help you in some way.
ઉપયોગી

usual *adjective*

Something that is **usual** is what happens most often.
સામાન્યપણે બનતું

*He arrived at his **usual** time.*

usually

If something **usually** happens, it is the thing that happens most often.
સામાન્ય રીતે

*I **usually** take the bus to school.*

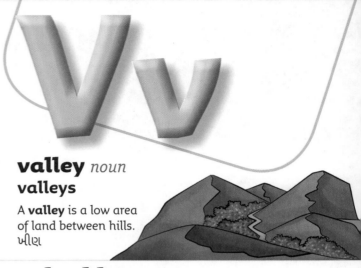

valley *noun*
valleys

A **valley** is a low area of land between hills.
ખીણ

valuable *adjective*

If something is **valuable**, it is worth a lot of money.
કીમતી

van *noun*
vans

A **van** is a covered vehicle larger than a car but smaller than a lorry. People use **vans** for carrying things.
વૅન - માલની હેરફેર માટેનું મધ્યમ કદનું વાહન

vase *noun*
vases

A **vase** is a jar for flowers.
ફૂલો સજાવવાનું પાત્ર

vegetable *noun*
vegetables

Vegetables are plants that you can cook and eat.
શાકભાજી

vehicle *noun*
vehicles

A **vehicle** is a machine that carries people or things from one place to another.
વાહન

verb *noun*
verbs

A **verb** is a word like 'sing,' 'feel,' or 'eat' that you use for saying what someone or something does.
ક્રિયાપદ

A
B
C
D
E
F
G
H
I
J
K
L
M
N
O
P
Q
R
S
T
U
V
W
X
Y
Z

very

Very is used before a word to make it stronger.
બહુ
*She had a **very** bad dream.*

vet *noun*
vets

A **vet** is a doctor for animals.
પશુચિકિત્સક

video *noun*
videos

A **video** is a copy of a film or television programme.
વિડિયો - વિડિયો ટેપ પર ઉતારેલી ફિલ્મ કે ટેલિવિઝન કાર્યક્રમ

village *noun*
villages

A **village** is a small town.
ગામડું

voice *noun*
voices

Your **voice** is the sound that comes from your mouth when you talk or sing.
સાદ, સૂર કે સ્વર,અવાજ

volcano *noun*
volcanoes

A **volcano** is a mountain that throws out hot, liquid rock and fire.
જ્વાળામુખી પર્વત

vote *verb*
votes, voting, voted

When a group of people **vote**, everybody shows what they want to do, usually by writing on a piece of paper or by putting their hands up.
મત
*We **voted** to send money to people who were in the earthquake.*

waist *noun*
waists

Your **waist** is the middle part of your body.
કમર

waist

wait *verb*
waits, waiting, waited

When you **wait** for something or someone, you spend time doing very little, before something happens.
રાહ જોવી

wake *verb*
wakes, waking, woke, woken

When you **wake** up, you stop sleeping.
ઊંઘીને ઉઠવું કે જાગવું

walk *verb*
walks, walking, walked

When you **walk**, you move along by putting one foot in front of the other.
ચાલવું

wall *noun*
walls

A **wall** is one of the sides of a building or a room.
ભીંત

want *verb*
wants, wanting, wanted

If you **want** something, you would like to have it.
...ની જરૂર હોવી

a b c d e f g h i j k l m n o p q r s t u v w x y z

A
B
C
D
E
F
G
H
I
J
K
L
M
N
O
P
Q
R
S
T
U
V
W
X
Y
Z

war noun
wars
A **war** is when countries or groups fight each other.
યુદ્ધ

wardrobe noun
wardrobes
A **wardrobe** is a tall cupboard that you can hang your clothes in.
પહેરવાના વસ્ત્રો ટાંગવાનો કબાટ

warm adjective
warmer, warmest
Something that is **warm** is not cold, but not hot.
માફકસરનું ગરમ, ઊનું
*The bread is still **warm** from the oven.*

warn verb
warns, warning, warned
If you **warn** someone about a possible problem or danger, you tell them about it.
સાવચેત કરવું
*I **warned** them not to go.*

was
➡ Look at **be**.
*It **was** my birthday yesterday.*

wash verb
washes, washing, washed
If you **wash** something, you clean it using soap and water.
(પાણી કે કોઈ પ્રવાહી વડે) ધોવું કે વીંછળવું

wasn't
Wasn't is short for **was not**.
ન હતું
*She **wasn't** happy.*

wasp noun
wasps
A **wasp** is an insect with wings and yellow and black stripes across its body. **Wasps** can sting people.
ઝેરી ડંખ મારનાર ભમરો કે ભમરી

waste verb
wastes, wasting, wasted
If you **waste** time, money, or energy, you use too much of it on something that is not important.
બગાડ કરવો, બગાડવું
*It's important not to **waste** water.*

watch verb
watches, watching, watched
If you **watch** something, you look at it for a period of time.
સતત નજર રાખવી

watch noun
watches
A **watch** is a small clock that you wear on your wrist.
કાંડા ઘડિયાળ

water noun
Water is a clear liquid that has no colour, taste or smell. It falls from clouds as rain.
પાણી

wave noun
waves
Waves on the surface of the sea are the parts that move up and down.
મોજું
*The **waves** broke over the rocks.*

wave verb
waves, waving, waved
If you **wave** your hand, you move it from side to side, usually to say hello or goodbye.
હાથ હલાવવો

wax *noun*

Wax is a soft material that melts when you make it hot. It is used to make crayons and candles.
મીણ

way *noun*
ways

1 A **way** of doing something is how you do it.
રીત
*This is the **way** to throw the ball.*

2 The **way** to a place is how you get there.
રસ્તો
*We're going the wrong **way**!*

weak *adjective*
weaker, weakest

If someone or something is **weak**, they are not strong.
નબળું
*When she spoke, her voice was **weak**.*

wear *verb*
wears, wearing, wore, worn

When you **wear** clothes, shoes or glasses, you have them on your body.
પહેરવું
*What are you going to **wear** today?*

weather *noun*

The **weather** is what it is like outside, for example if it is raining or sunny.
હવામાન
*What will the **weather** be like tomorrow?*

web *noun*
webs

1 The **Web** is made up of a very large number of websites all joined together. You can use it anywhere in the world to search for information.
વેબસાઈટ

2 A **web** is the thin net made by a spider from a string that comes out of its body.
જાળું

website *noun*
websites

A **website** is a place on the Internet that gives you information.
વેબસાઇટ - ઇન્ટરનેટ પર ઉપલબ્ધ એવી ચોક્કસ વિષય વિશેની માહિતી અને કાચી સામગ્રી

*Our school has a **website**.*

we'd

1 **We'd** is short for **we had**.
અમે કર્યું હતું
We'd left early in the morning.

2 **We'd** is also short for **we would**.
અમે કર્યું હતું
We'd like you to come with us.

wedding *noun*
weddings

A **wedding** is when two people get married.
લગ્નસમારંભ

Wednesday *noun*
Wednesdays

Wednesday is the day after Tuesday and before Thursday.
બુધવાર

week *noun*
weeks

A **week** is a period of seven days.
અઠવાડિયું
*This is the last **week** of the holidays.*

weekend *noun*
weekends

The **weekend** is the days at the end of the week, when you do not go to school or work.
રજા

weigh *verb*
weighs, weighing, weighed

If you **weigh** something or someone, you measure how heavy they are.
વજન કરવું

*I **weigh** more than my brother.*

a
b
c
d
e
f
g
h
i
j
k
l
m
n
o
p
q
r
s
t
u
v
w
x
y
z

weight *noun*

The **weight** of a person or thing is how heavy they are.
વજન
*What is your **weight** and height?*

well
better, best

If you do something **well**, you do it in a good way.
સારી રીતે
*He draws **well**.*

well *noun*

A **well** is a deep hole in the ground from which people take water, oil or gas.
કૂવો, વાવ

we'll

We'll is short for **we will**.
અમે કરીશું
We'll come along later.

went

⇨ Look at **go**.
*They **went** to school.*

were

⇨ Look at **be**.
*They **were** at home yesterday.*

we're

We're is short for **we are**.
અમે છીએ
We're late!

weren't

Weren't is short for **were not**.
અમે નહોતા
*They **weren't** at school yesterday.*

west *noun*

The **west** is the direction ahead of you when you are looking towards the place where the sun goes down.
પશ્ચિમ દિશા

wet *adjective*
wetter, wettest

If something is **wet**, it is covered in water.
ભીનું

we've

We've is short for **we have**.
અમારી પાસે છે
We've got lots of books.

whale *noun*
whales

Whales are very large sea mammals.
વ્હેલ માછલી
Whales breathe through a hole on the top of their heads.

what

You use **what** in questions when you ask for information.
શું
What time is it?

wheat *noun*

Wheat is a crop. People make flour and bread from **wheat**.
ઘઉં

wheel *noun*
wheels

Wheels are round and they turn. Bikes and cars move along on **wheels**.
પૈડું

wheelchair *noun*
wheelchairs

A **wheelchair** is a chair with wheels that you use if you cannot walk.
માંદાં કે અશક્ત લોકોની પૈડાંવાળી ખુરશી

when

You use **when** to ask what time something happened or will happen.
ક્યારે
When are you leaving?

where

You use **where** to ask questions about the place something is in.
ક્યાં
Where's your house?

which

You use **which** when you want help to choose between things.
કયું, કયા, કયો
Which shoes should I put on?

while

If one thing happens **while** another thing is happening, the two things are happening at the same time.
જ્યારે, ત્યારે
She goes to work while her children are at school.

whisper *verb*
whispers, whispering, whispered

When you **whisper**, you speak in a very quiet voice.
ગણગણવું
Don't you know it's rude to whisper?

whistle *verb*
whistles, whistling, whistled

When you **whistle**, you make sounds like music by blowing hard.
સીટી

white *noun*

White is the colour of snow or milk.
સફેદ રંગનું
His shirt is white.

who

You use **who** in questions when you ask about someone's name.
કોણ
Who won the quiz?

who'd

Who'd is short for **who would**.
કોને કરવું છે
Who'd like to come with me?

whole *adjective*

The **whole** of something is all of it.
આખું, બધું
Have the whole cake.

who'll

Who'll is short for **who will**.
કોણ કરશે
Who'll go and find her?

whose

You use **whose** to ask who something belongs to.
કોનું
Whose bag is this?

why

You use **why** when you are asking about the reason for something.
શા માટે, કેમ
Why did you do it?

wide *adjective*
wider, widest

Something that is **wide** is a large distance from one side to the other.
પહોળું
The bed is too wide for this room.

width *noun*

The **width** of something is the distance from one side to another.
પહોળાઈ
Measure the full width of the table.

wife *noun*
wives

A man's **wife** is the woman he is married to.
પત્ની

a b c d e f g h i j k l m n o p q r s t u v **w** x y z

A
B
C
D
E
F
G
H
I
J
K
L
M
N
O
P
Q
R
S
T
U
V
W
X
Y
Z

wild *adjective*
wilder, wildest

Wild animals or plants live or grow in nature, and people do not take care of them.
જંગલી

will *verb*

You use **will** to talk about things that are going to happen in the future.
સંભવિત હોવું
*Mum **will** be angry.*

win *verb*
wins, winning, won

If you **win**, you do better than everyone.
જીતવું
*You've **won** first prize!*

wind *noun*

Wind is air that moves.
પવન, વાયુ

wind *verb*
winds, winding, wound

1 If a road or river **winds**, it twists and turns.
વળતાં વળતાં જવું
2 When you **wind** something long around something, you wrap it around several times.
કશાકની આસપાસ વીંટવું
*She **wound** the rope around her waist.*

window *noun*
windows

A **window** is a space in the wall of a building or in the side of a vehicle that has glass in it.
બારી

wing *noun*
wings

The **wings** of birds, insects or aeroplanes are the parts that keep them in the air.
પાંખ

winner *noun*
winners

The **winner** of a race or competition is the person who wins it.
વિજેતા
*Our teacher will give the prizes to the **winners**.*

winter *noun*
winters

Winter is the season after autumn and before spring. In the **winter** the weather is usually cold.
શિયાળો

wipe *verb*
wipes, wiping, wiped

If you **wipe** dirt or liquid from something, you remove it using a cloth or your hands.
લૂછવું
*She **wiped** the tears from her eyes.*

wire *noun*
wires

A **wire** is a long thin piece of metal.
તાર
*The birds were sitting on a telephone **wire**.*

wise *adjective*
wiser, wisest

A **wise** person can decide on the right thing to do.
ડાહ્યું

wish *verb*
wishes, wishing, wished

If you **wish** something, you would like it to be true.
ઇચ્છા
*I **wish** I had a pet.*

witch *noun*
witches

In children's stories, a **witch** is a woman who has magic powers that she uses to do bad things.
ડાકણ

with

1 If one person is **with** another, they are together in one place.
-ની સાથે
*He's watching a film **with** his friends.*

2 You use **with** to say that someone has something.
વાળું
*My daughter is the girl **with** brown hair.*

without

If you do something **without** someone, they are not in the same place as you are, or they are not doing the same thing as you.
વગર, વિના
*He went **without** me.*

wives

⇨ Look at **wife**.
*The men bought flowers for their **wives**.*

wizard *noun*
wizards

In children's stories, a **wizard** is a man who has magic powers.
અસાધારણ શક્તિવાળી વ્યક્તિ

woke

⇨ Look at **wake**.
*They **woke** early.*

woken

⇨ Look at **wake**.
*We were **woken** by a loud noise.*

wolf *noun*
wolves

A **wolf** is a wild animal that looks like a large dog.
વરુ

woman *noun*
women

A **woman** is an adult female person.
સ્ત્રી

won

⇨ Look at **win**.
*She **won** first prize.*

won't

Won't is short for **will not**.
નહીં કરે
*I **won't** be late.*

wood *noun*
woods

1 **Wood** is the hard material that trees are made of.
લાકડું

2 A **wood** is a large area of trees growing near each other.
જંગલ

wool *noun*

Wool is a material made from the fur of sheep. It is used for making things such as clothes.
ઊન

word *noun*
words

Words are things that you say or write.
શબ્દ
*Some **words** are short and some are long.*

wore

⇨ Look at **wear**.
*She **wore** a red dress.*

work *verb*
works, working, worked

1 When you **work**, you do something that uses a lot of your time or effort.
નિયત કામ કરવું
*We **work** hard all day.*

2 If a machine **works**, it does its job.
કામ કરવું
*The TV isn't **working**.*

a
b
c
d
e
f
g
h
i
j
k
l
m
n
o
p
q
r
s
t
u
v
w
x
y
z

A
B
C
D
E
F
G
H
I
J
K
L
M
N
O
P
Q
R
S
T
U
V
W
X
Y
Z

world noun
worlds

The **world** is the earth, the planet we live on.
દુનિયા

worm noun
worms

A **worm** is a small animal with a long thin body, no bones, and no legs.
જીવડું

worn
➡ Look at **wear**.
*Have you **worn** this?*

worry verb
worries, worrying, worried

If you **worry**, you keep thinking about problems that you have or about nasty things that might happen.
ચિંતા કરવી

worse
If something is **worse** than another thing, it is not as good.
વધુ ખરાબ
*My spelling is **worse** than yours.*

worst
If something is the **worst**, all other things are better.
સૌથી ખરાબ
*That was the **worst** day in my life.*

worth
If something is **worth** a sum of money, that's how much you could sell it for.
અમુક કિંમતનું, ઉપયોગી, અગત્યનું
*This gold ring is **worth** a lot of money.*

would verb
You use **would** to say that someone agreed to do something. You use **would not** to say that they refused to do something.
થવાનું
*They said they **would** come to my party.*

wound
➡ Look at **wind**.
*She **wound** the rope around her wrist.*

wrap verb
wraps, wrapping, wrapped

When you **wrap** something, you fold paper or cloth around it to cover it.
વીટવું
*I didn't have enough paper to **wrap** the present.*

wrist noun
wrists

Your **wrist** is the part of your body between your arm and your hand. Your **wrists** bend when you move your hands.
કાંડું

write verb
writes, writing, wrote, written

When you **write** something, you use a pen or pencil to make letters, words, or numbers.
લખવું
*He **wrote** his name in the book.*

writing noun
Writing is words that have been written or printed.
લખાણ
*Can you read my **writing**?*

written
➡ Look at **write**.
*My uncle has **written** a song.*

wrong adjective
1 If you say that an answer is **wrong**, you mean that it is not right.
ખોટું
*No, you've got that **wrong**!*

2 If you say that something someone does is **wrong**, you mean that it is bad.
ખરાબ
*It is **wrong** to hurt animals.*

Xx

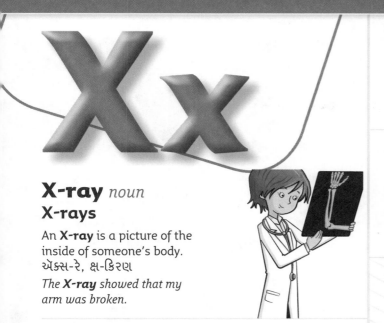

X-ray *noun*
X-rays

An **X-ray** is a picture of the inside of someone's body.
ઍક્સ-રે, ક્ષ-કિરણ

The X-ray showed that my arm was broken.

xylophone *noun*
xylophones

A **xylophone** is an instrument made of flat pieces of wood or metal in a row. You hit the pieces with a stick to make different sounds.
કાષ્ઠ-તરંગ

Yy

yacht *noun*
yachts

A **yacht** is a large boat with sails or an engine, used for races or for making trips.
યાટ- હલેસાં અથવા મોટરવાળી વિશાળ નૌકા, રેસ અથવા આનંદસફર કરવા તેનો ઉપયોગ થાય છે

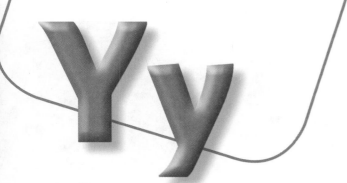

yawn *verb*
yawns, yawning, yawned

If you **yawn**, you open your mouth very wide and breathe in more air than usual because you are tired or bored.
બગાસું ખાવું

year *noun*
years

A **year** is a period of twelve months, beginning on January 1 and finishing on December 31.
વર્ષ

yell *verb*
yells, yelling, yelled

If you **yell**, you shout something, often because you are angry.
ચીસ, કિકિયારી

She yelled at him to stop.

yellow *noun*

Yellow is the colour of lemons or butter.
પીળા રંગનું

Her favourite colour is yellow.

yes

You say **yes** to agree with someone or to say that something is true, or if you want something.
હા!

yesterday

Yesterday is the day before today.
ગઇકાલે

There was no school yesterday.

yogurt or yoghurt *noun*
yogurts or **yoghurts**

Yogurt is a thick liquid food that is made from milk.
દહીં

I like strawberry yogurt more than peach yogurt.

yolk *noun*
yolks

The **yolk** of an egg is the yellow part.
ઈંડાની અંદરનો પીળો ભાગ, જરદી

you

You means the person or people that someone is talking or writing to.
તું, તમે

Can I help you?

a b c d e f g h i j k l m n o p q r s t u v w x y z

A
B
C
D
E
F
G
H
I
J
K
L
M
N
O
P
Q
R
S
T
U
V
W
X
Y
Z

you'd

1 **You'd** is short for **you had**.
તમે કર્યું છે
*I thought **you'd** told him.*

2 **You'd** is also short for **you would**.
તમે કરશો
You'd *like it a lot.*

you'll

You'll is short for **you will**.
તમે કરશો
You'll *be late!*

young *adjective*
younger, youngest

A **young** person, animal, or plant has not lived for very long.
યુવાન
*A kitten is a **young** cat.*

your

You use **your** to show that something belongs to the people that you are talking to.
તારું, તમારું (સગું સંબંધી)
*I do like **your** name.*

you're

You're is short for **you are**.
તમે છો
You're *very early!*

yours

Yours refers to something belonging to the people that you are talking to.
તારું, તમારું (માલિકીનું)
*His hair is longer than **yours**.*

yourself
yourselves

Yourself means you alone.
તમે જાતે, તમે પોતે જ
*You'll hurt **yourself**.*

you've

You've is short for **you have**.
તમારી પાસે છે
You've *got very long legs.*

zebra *noun*
zebras

A **zebra** is a wild African animal like a horse with black and white stripes.
ઝીબ્રા-ઘોડા જેવું સફેદ અને કાળી પટ્ટીઓવાળું આફ્રિકન પ્રાણી

zero
zeros or zeroes

Zero is the number .
શૂન્ય

zip *noun*
zips

A **zip** is two long rows of little teeth and a piece that slides along them. You pull this to open or close the **zip**.
દાંતાવાળા બે પડ કે બાજુઓને એકબીજા સાથે જોડીને બંધ

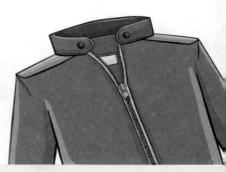

zoo *noun*
zoos

A **zoo** is a place where live animals are kept so that people can look at them.
પ્રાણીસંગ્રહાલય